Grill Italian

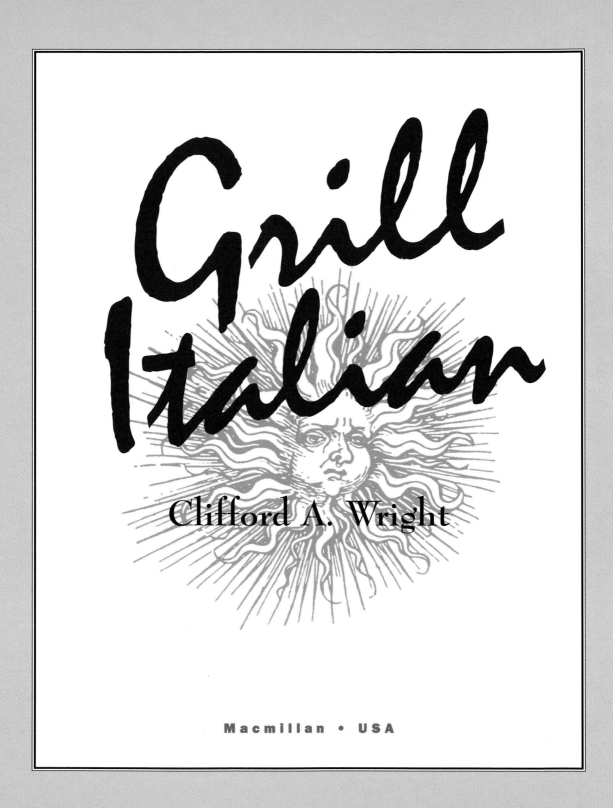

Grill Italian

Clifford A. Wright

Macmillan • USA

MACMILLAN
A Simon & Schuster Macmillan Company
1633 Broadway
New York, NY 10019

Library of Congress Cataloging-in-Publication Data
Wright, Clifford A.
    Grill Italian : 100 classic recipes alla griglia / Clifford A. Wright
        p.   cm.
    Includes index.
    ISBN: 0-02-860365-6 (alk. Paper)
    1. Barbecue cookery.   2. Cookery, Italian.   I. Title.
TX840.B3W75   1996   95-35424
641.5'784'0945—dc20   CIP

Designer: Nick Anderson
Photographer: Dennis M. Gottlieb
Food Stylist: William L. Smith
Prop Stylist: Denise Canter

Manufactured in the United States of America

10 9 8 7 6 5 4 3 2 1

For the guys, grill on: Boyd Grove,
David Forbes, Eric Stange, Mark Chalek,
Kanaan Makiya, Harry Irwin, Stephan Haggard

Contents

Acknowledgments

The pure conviviality of grilling makes a book on grilling Italian food the best of all possible worlds for a writer and cook. I had my grills fired up for months on end, testing and retesting and having a grand time with my friends. Thanks to Mark Chalek, Jenny Lavigne, Harry Irwin, Pam Haltom, David Forbes, Ginny Sherwood, Eric Stange, Barbara Costa, and all their children for sharing the food and good times.

I also want to thank my agent, Doe Coover, and my editors, Jane Sigal and Pam Hoenig, for their enthusiastic support and wise suggestions.

1

Introduction to Italian-Style Grilling

A fire blazing away, red-hot coals, the scent of sizzling steak wafting through the still air: there is nothing quite like the first barbecue of summer. Out come the perennial American favorites—hamburgers, hot dogs, ribs. But before too long we're looking for new ideas and exciting flavors to cook on the grill. And we can find them by turning to America's favorite cuisine—Italian.

My own memories of grilled Italian food are what prompted me to write this book. I fondly remember a grilled dinner in San Gregorio in Sicily, overlooking the azure waters of the Tyrrhenian Sea. The restaurant, La Tartaruga, arranged its white-clothed tables randomly about an awning-covered terra-cotta piazza. The sea breeze cooled the hot air of the late summer day. In the center of the restaurant was a large, square, wood-fired oven and grill station. I ordered a riso di mare to start, a rice salad cooked al dente and flecked with the tiniest bits of smoked salmon, mussels, tuna, shrimp, parsley, clams, squid, caviar, carrots, and hearts of palm. Everything was so finely chopped and delicate—it was an elegant and perfect accompaniment to the grilled skewers of grouper and anchovy that arrived shortly.

Next came the *secondo,* a main course of *spiedini di acciuga e cernia.* Here the chef had delicately boned and butterflied (butterflying a fish means to remove the backbone while leaving the fillets attached) fresh anchovies along with thin grouper fillets. They were lightly seasoned and rolled up, dredged in bread crumbs, and skewered before being grilled slowly to a golden brown and drizzled with olive oil. The warm breeze lifted the awning upward, the smoke swirled from the grill, and I suddenly realized that this was heaven—simple Italian food grilled and eaten outdoors.

At home, anytime I grill Italian food, I try to re-create the leisurely al fresco dining experience I remember from my journeys in Italy.

The grill cuisine of Italy is about freshness, simplicity, and intense natural flavors: succulent shrimp grilled to inviting orange perfection (*scampi alla griglia*) is just one example. Italian-style grilling is also about Italy's aromatic ingredients—olive oil, oregano, rosemary, prosciutto, pancetta, and pecorino, to name a few—and the way Italian cooks typically combine these ingredients on the grill. Thin scallopine of pork tenderloin stuffed with bread crumbs and herbs, called *involtini di maiale* in Italy, grilled slowly with a basting sauce of fruity olive oil flavored with garlic and oregano, could have come only from the repertoire of an Italian cook.

The range of grilled Italian dishes is exciting too. Swordfish seared with a latticework design and bathed in a warm olive oil, garlic, and oregano sauce, called *sammurigghiu,* is a favorite of my guests. Friends often ask me to make *àrista* (although they ask in English), a whole boneless pork loin with rosemary, stuffed with garlic and parsley, slowly spit-roasted and basted with rosemary-infused olive oil. Skewered and grilled foods, such as a Sicilian recipe of kebabs with sausage, orange slices, onions, and bay leaf, are always popular with family and friends.

These preparations and many more are perennial Italian favorites, yet they are hardly known in this country, even with our love of Italy's cuisine. In restaurants throughout the country, we find all kinds of inventions and fads appearing on the grill as customers demand to be wowed somehow or other. But we don't need to be novel when it comes to the Italian grill. Here is a cuisine that has stood the test of time. The repertoire of authentic and traditional Italian grill preparations is a fabulous storehouse of delicious recipes waiting for the adventurous cook.

The roots of grilling in Italy, as everywhere else, go back to Neolithic times. But cooking, *alla griglia,* on the grill, a method that was always considered primitive, became popular when restaurants in Italy began to use it in the nineteenth century. Grilling became even more popular in Italy a couple of decades after World War II, when, as in America, incomes rose and lifestyles became more carefree. Middle-class Italians in densely populated areas began to grill not out of necessity, as rural folk traditionally had, but as a fun, leisure activity.

The term *alla griglia* is used to describe foods that are grilled over charcoal or wood. The word *grigliata* refers to a platter of grilled foods, meat, fish, or vegetables, usually three to four or more kinds of one or the other. In Italy food is also grilled on a *graticola,* a ridged cast-iron pan or griddle, or on a *gratella,* a grilling grate made of iron. Cooking *ai ferri* means grilling over embers or cooking in a cast-iron pan. *Alla brace* means cooking directly in the embers or on a grilling grate.

A *girarrosto* is a spit, or rotisserie, and the device that turns it. Normally food is spit-roasted over a wood fire, and in the old days the *girarrosto* was devised like a piece of clockwork or driven by a blindfolded animal walking around and around. Today it is rare for homes to have one, and when they do, it usually is an attachment inside the oven. Many American-made grills have an electric rotisserie accessory that is fine for spit-roasting. If you have one, give it a try. I think you'll be pleased with the results.

Spit-roasting is such a delightful way to cook that I believe a rotisserie should be integral to a grill, not merely an accessory. Spit-roasting is a common method of grilling large meats and whole birds in Italy, so I have included several recipes using the method later in the book.

Italians are so fond of grilling that many homes have built-in brick fireplaces where the cook can prepare platters of mixed grilled meats, grilled roll-ups of meat or fish, and grilled mixed vegetables. In Italy a wide variety of foods—whole fish, fish steaks, shellfish, chicken, duck, game, beef, veal, pork, lamb, rabbit, variety meats, songbirds, and many vegetables—are grilled in a variety of ways.

Many millennia ago, someone purposely placed a piece of meat over an open fire and had the first grill. It wasn't a barbecue. This is a point to make before getting into the grill cuisine of the Italians. The word *barbecue* (or *barbeque*) is often used incorrectly by both Americans and Italians to mean grilling. In fact barbecuing is a method of slowly cooking over a covered fire utilizing low heat and smoke.

This book is about grilling Italian style, and I will use the word *grilling* throughout. *Grilling* means cooking directly over or in a wood or charcoal fire or over stone briquets heated by a gas-fired grill.

Italians grill in a manner similar to that of Americans, but one will find more permanent means for grilling in Italy: built-in fireplaces for cooking are not unusual, and spit-roasting devices are common as well. We can learn many things from the Italians about grilled foods. But one of my favorite grill stories is about the time General Dwight D. Eisenhower taught an Italian how to cook a steak. Gene Leone, son of the famous Mama Leone, whose restaurant in New York was an upscale emporium of Italian cooking in the 1920s, tells the story of a West Point class of 1915 reunion at which he and Generals Eisenhower and Omar Bradley stood around the grill and followed Eisenhower's suggestion to sprinkle 2-inch-thick prime sirloin steaks with salt and pepper and throw them directly into the wood charcoal fire. It worked, and you can try it too.

Now let's move on to some basics about grilling, namely grills, fuel, fire, accessories, and the grill pantry.

Grills

Your grill is the most important piece of equipment for grilling. I will not make brand recommendations but will inform you that all the recipes in the book were tested on the three grills I have: a Weber kettle grill, a Ducane 2002S gas grill with rotisserie attachment, and an outdoor brick fireplace for natural hardwood fires. This book assumes you are grilling with either a hooded gas grill or a covered charcoal kettle grill such as the one made by Weber.

Other grill possibilities are in-ground stone-lined pit barbecues, braziers, hibachis, uncovered grill carts, wagon grills, spit-roasting grills, and some others.

When shopping for a grill, look for heavy, solid construction, such as a firebox (also called a burner box or grilling box, this is the part that holds the heat source) made of heavy-duty cast aluminum. For gas grills, avoid paying a lot of money for useless bells and whistles such as windows, timers, fuel gauges (just keep a spare tank handy), and temperature gauges. Before buying an assortment of accessories for your grill, read the section on page 13.

For safety, read all the manufacturer's instructions before using a gas grill. Remember that you are using fire, so use common sense too. Both gas and charcoal grills produce carbon monoxide, so always use them outdoors, not in an enclosed area. Keep the grill more than a foot away from combustible materials. Store your spare LP gas (propane) tank away from the grill outdoors. Manufacturers' manuals, dealers, and propane gas dealers can all instruct you on the proper way to attach the tank to the grill gas hose.

All propane gas grill regulators must meet U.S. Department of Transportation regulations and will be equipped with a quick connective plug allowing you to make fast and totally safe hookups between your grill and propane tank. Gas only flows when the plug is properly connected by being fully engaged into the coupling. When you are finished grilling, remember to turn off the grill control knobs first, then the valve of the propane tank.

Uncovered grills such as hibachis and portable braziers are not recommended for grilling Italian food for a variety of reasons that I go into on page 7. Any serious griller will either already have or will purchase one of the two types of grills recommended; that is, a charcoal grill with a cover or a gas grill with a cover.

The only other possibility is an indoor fireplace grill, or what is called a Tuscan fireplace grill, which can be used in an open-hearth fireplace. I became fascinated with the idea of having a built-in indoor grill in my next home or my dream house when I saw how easy (sort of) it is to build.

A few years ago I rented a room in a top-floor apartment in a palazzo in Venice. My Italian roommate-owners decided to have an indoor grill installed, and I watched the mason build it, without blueprints, using only his imagination. It didn't take him very long to complete, and having grilled foods year round was a real attraction.

But to get back to reality—the reason for a covered grill is that you can control your fire better and capture the smoke that makes food flavorful. The most common charcoal grill is a covered kettle grill of the type Weber makes. The cover and the firebox both have adjustable vent holes used to control the heat. Because neither the coals in the firebox nor the grilling grid are movable (meaning the food is always 5 to 10 inches away from the heat source), the only way to control the heat is by using the vents and cover or by building the charcoal fire to the side.

The other kind of grill that I recommend is the gas grill. For years I derided gas grills. I argued that you couldn't possibly make real grilled food with one, that only a charcoal fire gave you real grilled taste. Then I rented a house on Cape Cod one summer and it was equipped with a gas grill, which I lamented upon seeing. Two weeks later, after grilling with ease and to my heart's content, I became a convert and will extol the not-inconsiderable virtues of the gas grill: it's easy to fire up; a top-quality grill such as Ducane barely needs to be cleaned; it takes only 15 to 20 minutes to preheat, versus 30 to 40 minutes to get a fire going; you don't mess with dirty coals; and there are no ashes to remove.

And what about the food? Well, this is the key point. The reason food tastes good when grilled is not because of the fuel source but because fat drips down on hot coals or lava rocks and returns in the form of smoke to flavor the food.

There is one big drawback to gas grills: they never get as hot as a charcoal or wood fire. I find this annoying occasionally. Gas grillers complain that charcoal grills require lighter fuel, which gives the food a gasoline taste. But this isn't true—unless you put food on before the fuel has burned off.

In the end, if you are in the market for a grill and are trying to decide between gas or charcoal, the only strategy is to compare the pros and cons.

The pro argument for a gas grill is ease of use and cleaning. The pro argument for a charcoal grill is a hotter fire than a gas grill and perhaps the elemental satisfaction of building a fire. In either case, when shopping for a grill, don't be cheap. Get the best—it will last.

All grilling grates (also called grids or grills) can be cleaned by burning off the food at high temperatures or by quickly scraping them directly after grilling while they are still hot. It is important that the grates be clean, but remember that the grates will clean while the grill is preheating. I have never cleaned the grates of my grills with scrubbers or chemical cleaners. I simply burn off all food particles and grease with a high-temperature fire and scrape it into the fire below with a long-handled spatula.

The grill grates can be oiled before grilling, and you can also oil your food to prevent sticking. The ideal grate is a thick, heavy cast-iron grate, which unfortunately is not made for any commercial gas or charcoal grill that I know of.

Fuel

The big debate about fuel for grill fires is among gas, lump hardwood charcoal, and charcoal briquets.

To my mind, the debate is spurious for several reasons. The keys to good grilled food will always be the expertise and imagination of the cook, the love he or she has for shopping for, preparing, and cooking good food, and the quality of the ingredients used. There are differences, of course, between gas and charcoal, and some people will prefer one over the other, but in the end, the equipment and fuel are not as important as the food being grilled and the mastery of the cook.

Let's talk about charcoal. Traditionalists say charcoal produces better flavor than gas. They favor natural lump hardwood charcoal over charcoal briquets, which contain chemicals and may require starter fluid. I have three points to make about this controversy.

First, charcoal briquets and lighter fluids do have chemicals in them. Charcoal absorbs odors and gases, which is why it is used as a filter in everything from cigarettes to gas masks to deep-fryers. Yet here's the thing to remember (it's worth repeating): These chemicals can affect the food you are grilling, but only if you have placed the food on the grill before the charcoal is red hot, that is, before the charcoal briquets have had a chance to burn off the lighter fluid and other chemicals.

Second, the flavor of grilled food is produced by fat and juices dripping on hot coals or hot lava rocks, as I have also said before. The flavors come not from the fuel source but from the fats of the food being grilled.

Third, charcoal briquets are inexpensive and easily found in stores. Any toxins that might possibly enter the human system as a result of using charcoal briquets are probably, over a lifetime, about the same as would be found in the environment anyway.

There are several basic kinds of fuel available for charcoal grills:

Charcoal briquets are processed pieces of charcoal formed into shapes. They may contain coal and chemicals to make them easier and quicker to light and burn. Charcoal briquets are the most common fuel, easy to find, inexpensive, and easily stored.

Natural lump hardwood charcoal is unprocessed lumps of charcoal from wood that has been burned by smoldering. The woods used are usually hardwoods such as oak or maple. Lump charcoal is expensive and hard to find but produces a very hot fire that stays hot longer. If I had my choice, I would always choose lump hardwood charcoal over all other fuel sources. I don't mainly because it's hard to find. I have, however, uncovered a mail-order source: Nature's Own Charcoal, (800) 289-2427.

Mesquite charcoal is simply a natural lump charcoal made from mesquite trees and shrubs of Mexico and the American Southwest. Its use is not really appropriate for Italian-style grilling because it lends an uncharacteristic flavor to the food.

Natural wood is used especially if you want smoke. Kiln-dried maple, oak, and hickory are ideal; they burn much hotter than seasoned wood. It is important when making a wood fire not to use woods, such as pine or fir, that give off resinous fumes, which might spoil the food. Never use composite woods, such as plywood, for cooking. In Italy you will find olive wood, grapevine clippings, orange wood, and various shrubs used for fuel.

Wood chips, such as cherry, apple, or hickory, are sold in small packages and are used for enhancing the flavors in both charcoal and gas grill fires by creating smoke. Two handfuls of wood chips are soaked in water first and then thrown around the average fire. Gas grills usually have a small receptacle where you can put the chips. Rather than pay high prices for these wood chips, you can do as the Italians do and save herb twigs, nut shells, garlic heads, or any other aromatic and use them on the fire.

Olive briquets are a new product on the market. They are made from ground olive pits, olive pulp, and olive oil. They are placed on red hot coals or in the receptacle of a preheated gas grill with the cover down. They can be ordered from Infood, (201) 569-3073.

Propane gas: *See* page 6.

Charcoal lighter fuel: I'm not a fan of charcoal lighter fuel, but for all its drawbacks, lighter fuel gets a charcoal fire going. Anybody who complains about the smell and taste of gasoline on the food is either a very lousy cook or someone who has eaten the food of a very lousy cook. The whole idea behind lighter fuel is to get a charcoal fire going, not to cook with it. You must let the fuel burn off before you start cooking. Never start grilling when flames are still visible, only when each and every charcoal is completely white with ash. A better bet than lighter fuel is a metal flue or fire can (described below).

Fire

Preparing a charcoal fire: The most effective method of preparing a charcoal fire without a fire can is to mound the charcoal in the center of the firebox or to one side, or to make two mounds on each side, leaving the center empty. But you will need lighter fuel to start the fire. The idea is to have some part of the grill much cooler than the other so that you can move food around to less intense heat. If you are grilling food that is fatty, such as a duck, mounding the charcoal on two sides and setting a drip pan in the center works very well.

For starting charcoal fires quickly, try using a fire can instead of lighter fuel. The coals are piled into the can and lit with the help of two sheets of

---

How Hot Is a Hot Charcoal Fire?

Gas grills have burner control knobs with high, medium, and low settings, and although they are generally inaccurate, the settings are useful as guides. The recipes in this book instruct you to preheat your gas grill on one or another of these settings, but what are you to do if you are using a charcoal grill? This is a bit more difficult.

The heat of a charcoal fire will depend on how many coals you have used, how you have mounded or spread them, and other factors. In all cases the heat from a charcoal fire will be variable, and you should be aware of this when you cook, using the times I give in the recipes with a dose of common sense.

The Weber grill instruction manual suggests 25 briquets for a 22-inch-diameter grill cooking food for one hour. I find this too few coals, but if you were to follow their instructions, you would have what I call a "low" or "slow" charcoal fire. Generally a "hot" charcoal fire is one with the coals about 5 to 6 inches beneath the grilling grate; the food is cooked directly above the coals. For a "medium" charcoal fire the coals are mounded to one side of the grill firebox, 5 to 6 inches beneath the grilling grate, and the food is cooked on the cool side of the grill, where there are no coals. A "low" fire is the same as a "medium" fire except fewer coals are used and the food is cooked as far away as possible from the coals.

This might seem very inaccurate, and it is; that's the nature of the grilling beast, and the reason for it being so much fun. This is a hands-on experience for both expert and novice griller.

rolled-up newspaper. When the briquets are ready, they are dumped into the firebox. You can also use only newspaper to get your fire going, but do not use loose sheets because the pieces can fly about and cause fires. Roll newspapers up very tightly, like branches, before using them for kindling. Or you can use lighter fuel (but see what I have to say about this on page 10). Liberally douse the charcoal and set on fire at three different points. It will blaze a while, then the flames will die out. Do not add more lighter fuel when this happens—it is not necessary since the briquets are now lit and will burn slowly. You can leave the charcoal to burn until it is ready for grilling in 35 to 40 minutes, when all of the coals are completely covered with white ash. Knock the ash off and push the coals around a bit to cover a large grilling area, leaving some room for a cool spot, then start grilling food.

Heat can be regulated by opening and closing the vents on the bottom of the charcoal grill's firebox or the vents on top of the cover (if your grill cover has them), by lowering and raising the grilling grate (if your grill has adjustable grates), and by closing or opening the cover.

Some supermarkets sell lightable charcoal briquet bags. These bags—about 2½ to 5 pounds of charcoal, enough for one grill fire—are placed in the firebox and both ends of the bag are lit, so there is no lighter fluid or pyramiding of briquets involved. They really are very easy and convenient. This is my preferred method when I am not grilling by gas or wood and when the total grilling time is less than 20 minutes.

Some charcoal briquets are soaked in lighter fuel and can simply be mounded and fired up with only a match.

When you are finished grilling, close all the vents on the cover of the grill and the coals will slowly stop burning. Knock the ashes off and you will be able to save a number of partly used coals for a future fire.

Preparing a wood fire: I learned to do this in Boy Scouts. At one jubilee I participated in, I had 3 minutes to build a fire from scratch, without newspapers or lighter fuel, using no more than three matches, to burn through a string suspended 14 inches above the ground. I can still do this, but you can take your time.

Starting a good fire revolves around well-seasoned wood kindling of different sizes. Kindling can be found lying around the ground everywhere—if it bends instead of snapping, don't use it. Children, thankfully, love snooping around and collecting firewood kindling. Start by building a little teepee of crackly twigs that are about $1/16$ inch in diameter. Around this base arrange slightly larger twigs, say $1/8$ inch thick, then a layer of $1/4$-inch twigs. Light the innermost, thinnest twigs, and as the fire starts to build, add one or two branches $1/2$ to 1 inch in diameter. Do not add wood too fast, because until coals form, you will have a fire that will go out. Keep adding wood as you see the need until you've got a roaring blaze. Now keep your eyes open for the coals forming, placing logs on top of the fire. After about an hour you can begin grilling, although some preparations, such as the Sardinian Roast Suckling Pig on page 33, will require many hours of coal formation.

Preheating a gas grill: The recipes will instruct you to preheat the gas grill on a particular setting for 15 minutes. This is easy enough. Just remember not to start grilling until the grill is preheated; otherwise your food will be unappetizing.

Grilling Accessories

The following are the most important tools for grilling:

Basting brush: Many grilled foods need to be basted before or during cooking. A long-handled brush is ideal. Dedicate a 2-inch-wide paint brush for larger pieces of meat.

Bulb suction baster: The kind of bulb baster you use for basting the Thanksgiving turkey makes collecting the juices in aluminum drip pans much easier. Some recipes, including all the spit-roasting preparations, utilize drip pans placed in the center of a charcoal grill (with coals mounded on either side) or under a rack placed on a gas grill's grating to collect the drippings used for basting, which provide the crucial flavor and taste to Italian-style grilling.

Fire-starter cans or metal flues: A nice alternative to lighter fuel, fire-starter cans are shaped like a coffee can with a handle and have holes around the bottom for ventilation. You pile up the coals inside over rolled-up newspaper. The whole effect is like a blast furnace.

Fish grills or fish baskets: Because fish is more delicate than meat, hinged fish-shaped baskets can be used to enclose whole fish for grilling and turning. They must be oiled before using, but I think the grill topper (described below) works better for fish.

Grill basket: This hinged square-shaped basket can be used for grilling small foods or pieces of food. Like the grill topper (below), grill baskets are useful for cooking vegetables. You can also toss the vegetables by shaking, which you can't do with a grill topper.

Grill topper: Usually a perforated sheet of metal, a grill topper holds foods that would otherwise fall through the grilling grate. It is excellent for cooking whole fish, fish that flakes, small vegetables, and other small foods like unskewered shrimp or scallops.

Hot pads or pot holders: Keep a couple of pot holders near your grill—you'll be surprised how often you need them at a critical moment.

Lighter sticks: Useful for lighting fires.

Long tongs: An essential tool, long tongs are used for turning skewers and any other food except fish. Never use forks for grilling; all they do is puncture food.

Meat thermometer: Useful for taking the internal temperature of large meats.

Rotisserie: A rotisserie is an essential accessory for spit-roasting. Most grill manufacturers sell electrically driven rotisserie attachments. The key to successful spit-roasting, the finest way to really roast (roasting in an oven is a misnomer because it's actually baking), is to make absolutely sure the piece of meat or bird is attached securely and evenly onto the spit. If it is not secure, it will spin and never turn. If the weight is unbalanced, the spit will turn a little too fast and the food will cook unevenly.

Roto-kebabs: These kebab-holding racks have one handle for turning multiple kebabs.

Skewers: You can use either metal or wooden skewers. Metal ones are best for things like shish kebab. For grilled Italian foods I prefer wooden skewers. Skewering is often done with a double set of skewers to keep the food from turning on the skewer and to provide for easier handling. The ends of the skewers may burn if your fire is very hot. You can retard this by covering the ends with aluminum foil or soaking the skewers in water for 15 minutes first. Or let them burn off and remove the remaining skewer before serving.

Spatula: A spatula is indispensable, either a long-handled grilling spatula or a professional long-bladed offset spatula, which is ideal for turning larger pieces of fish or whole small fish. Never use a rubber or wooden spatula when grilling.

Grill thermometers: An individual meat or poultry thermometer for a roast or bird can be useful, but grill thermometers are usually inaccurate.

Water: If a fire starts to get out of control, you put it out by turning off the gas or covering the firebox. It is wise to keep a hose nearby in case of a more serious fire.

Wire brush for cleaning: Why bother? Just let the intense heat do the cleaning—it's the same principle as a self-cleaning oven.

The Italian Grill Pantry

The following section is not a full accounting of all the foods you will be using, many of which are explained in the recipes, but a short listing of some ingredients I believe are important to grilled Italian food.

Anchovies (cured): The best anchovies are the salted whole anchovies sold from tin barrels in Italian grocery markets. Salted anchovies are used as a condiment for cooking in Italian cuisine. They are an essential flavor in Italian cuisine and are never optional.

Bread crumbs: Use only unseasoned dry bread crumbs unless fresh bread crumbs, which can be made with fresh or slightly stale bread, are specified.

Bread cubes: In a number of skewered recipes, bread cubes are used to divide meat or vegetables. A long Italian loaf or French baguette is cut up, including the crust, into 1-inch cubes.

Caciocavallo: A firm cheese made from cow's milk and shaped like a spindle, caciocavallo can be found in Italian markets. Caciocavallo can be replaced with provolone.

Caul fat: The omentum, or caul fat, is a membrane-like fatty net that surrounds the stomach. Translucent, almost transparent, it is very fragile and must be unraveled and spread out with great care so that it doesn't rip. In Italy caul fat is used like a sausage skin to enclose food. Because of its fat, it acts as a self-baster, good for lean foods such as Tuscan-Style Grilled Liver in Caul Fat (page 84). In supermarket meat departments you usually have to ask for pork caul fat, since the word *omentum* is not generally known. It may be necessary for the butcher to order it for you. Also check with Greek markets, which often have caul fat around holiday times.

Chickens: Free-range or semi-free-range chickens are best in flavor and color. These chickens are allowed to wander freely, feeding as they move about. As a result, they taste significantly better than the industrial chickens of Misters Tyson and Perdue, with their genetically absurd breasts and bodies, although they are more expensive.

Fat back: *See* pork fat.

Lard: Melted lard is often used for basting in traditional Italian grill recipes. I know lard is unpopular today, but if you want an authentic, memorable taste, use it—it is a flavoring. You don't actually eat a lot of lard because most of it drips off. Lard is sold in supermarkets either near the butter or near the bacon.

Lemons: Always use freshly squeezed lemon juice, never bottled. The tastes are not comparable.

Mortadella: The Italian name for bologna is mortadella. The domestic brand made by Citterio is very good. It is available in Italian markets and many supermarket delicatessens.

Pancetta: Sometimes called Italian bacon, pancetta is cured (not smoked like American bacon) pork belly, most often found rolled into a cylinder. It usually can be found in an Italian market. If you can't find it, use slab bacon parboiled for 10 minutes.

Parsley: The recipes use flat-leaf parsley, which I find less bitter than curly leaf.

Pecorino: A hard Italian grating cheese made from sheep's milk, pecorino is easily found—ask the supermarket manager if you don't see it. Pecorino crotonese is a 90-day-old pecorino sometimes called an "eating" pecorino. It is found in Italian markets and is generally used at the table rather than in cooking.

Pork fat: Pork fat is used as a tenderizer or flavoring agent for some preparations and for making sausages. It can be trimmed from fatty pieces of meat, or you can use pork fat back or even salt pork, in which case you may not need to use any more salt. Pork fat back and salt pork are sold in supermarkets, usually near the bacon; otherwise, ask the butcher.

Prosciutto: Domestically produced prosciutto is fine for cooking. Imported prosciutto has an amazing taste and melts in your mouth, but it is very expensive.

Olive oil: Unless specified otherwise, "olive oil" in a recipe refers to an inexpensive extra-virgin olive oil.

Rabbit: A great-tasting "white" meat. My children, who eat rabbit and who have noticed the unpleasant taste of industrial chickens (see above), say that rabbit tastes better, even the frozen ones.

Soppressata: Lightly smoked and pressed (hence the name), soppressata is a dried sausage made of coarsely chopped pork, pancetta, or bacon; wine; and sometimes pig's blood and paprika to give it a red color. It is available in Italian markets or can be replaced with salami.

Variety meats: This term refers to various innards popular in Italian cooking, such as liver, heart, sweetbreads, kidneys, and brains. Keep an open mind and your tastes will expand too. Remember that nonallergic food aversions are cultural and psychological, not physiological. Generally, variety meats can be found in supermarkets, although you may have to ask the butcher to order it.

The Recipes

2

Grilled Meats

Grilled Pork Rolls with Bread Crumbs and Lamb Liver

"Involtini di Maiale alla Griglia"

Italians love various meat roll-ups, called involtini, *skewered and cooked on the grill. In this preparation pork is stuffed with finely chopped aromatic ingredients and skewered. The involtini grill slowly and are finished when the bread just begins to blacken.*

If feeding children, leave out the liver, which I believe they find too strong a taste. The pork fat used in the stuffing helps tenderize the meat and adds flavor.

1 cup fresh bread crumbs

$1/2$ cup milk

1 garlic clove, peeled and finely chopped

$1/2$ cup finely chopped fresh parsley

$1/4$ cup finely chopped pork fat

2 tablespoons finely chopped lamb, pork, veal, or chicken liver

1 large egg, beaten

Salt and freshly ground black pepper

$1 1/2$ pounds pork tenderloin, cut into twenty $1/2$-inch-thick slices

1. Prepare a medium-hot charcoal fire or preheat a gas grill for 15 minutes on medium.

2. Soak the bread crumbs in the milk and then squeeze the milk out with your hands and discard the milk. Place the soaked bread crumbs, the garlic, parsley, pork fat, and liver in a medium-size mixing bowl and mix well. Add the egg and salt and pepper to taste, then mix again.

3. Place the pork slices between 2 pieces of wax paper and flatten with a mallet or the side of a heavy cleaver until they are about 4 × 3-inch scallopine.

4. Spread the stuffing on the pork slices and roll them up, folding the edges in and securing with a toothpick if necessary. Shape and squeeze in the palms of your hands so the stuffing does not escape. Freeze any leftover stuffing.

About ¹/₂ loaf Italian or French bread, cut into twenty 1-inch cubes

Ten 8-inch wooden skewers

Olive oil for drizzling

5. Put 2 *involtini* on each skewer interspersed with 2 bread cubes per skewer. Drizzle olive oil over the meat and bread.

6. Place the *involtini* on the grill and cook, turning occasionally, until the bread just begins to blacken, about 30 minutes.

Makes 4 to 6 servings

Grilled Skewered Pork with Prosciutto and Sage

"Spiedini di Maiale"

Pork tenderloin is a buttery cut of meat ideal for grilling and with the bread is a natural foil for the aromatic flavors of fresh sage and prosciutto. A drizzle of olive oil at the end keeps the meat and bread moist and glistening. The double skewer keeps the ingredients from sliding and helps them cook more evenly.

Sixteen 10-inch wooden skewers

1 3/4 pounds pork tenderloin, cut into twenty-four 1-inch-thick cubes

About 1/2 loaf French or Italian bread, cut into twenty-four 1-inch cubes

Twenty-four 1/8-inch-thick squares of sliced prosciutto (about 6 ounces)

24 fresh sage leaves

Olive oil for drizzling

Salt and freshly ground black pepper

1. Prepare a hot charcoal fire or preheat a gas grill for 15 minutes on high.

2. Double skewer all the ingredients: hold 2 skewers parallel to each other about 1/2 inch apart between your thumb and forefinger. Pierce a cube of pork with the double skewer, followed by a piece of bread, prosciutto, and sage. Repeat until all the ingredients are skewered. You should have 3 pieces of each ingredient per double skewer.

3. Drizzle each double skewer with olive oil. Salt and pepper on both sides to taste and grill until the bread and pork are golden brown, about 15 minutes per side.

Makes 8 skewers, or 6 servings

Variation: The sage can be replaced with bay leaves that have been soaked in hot water for 30 minutes to make them less brittle. In Rome they call this preparation (without the bay leaves) *lombello*, a dialect word for tenderloin, and they brush the meat with melted lard while grilling.

Grilled Pork Chops over Soft Rolls

"Panuntella"

"*Greased bread*"—*that's the literal meaning of* panuntella. *But this exceedingly simple preparation from the region of Lazio, where Rome is the capital, produces not grease, but brilliantly flavored grilled pork chops on grilled bread. The pork chops are placed on a rack over the bread, which catches the drippings while the pork slowly grills.*

The key to success, though, involves two things: first, the pork chops must have a nice ring of fat around them, and second, you will want to prevent the bread from becoming dried out and brittle before the meat cooks. I explain how in the directions. Soft, chewy rolls, sliced open, or a soft, dense white bread with the crust removed works best.

6 thick pork chops with some fat on them (2 1/2 to 3 pounds total)

1/4 cup melted lard

Salt and freshly ground black pepper

3 thick, chewy soft rolls, sliced open; or six 1-inch-thick slices good-quality white bread, crusts removed, a little larger than the pork chops

1. Prepare a hot charcoal fire or preheat a gas grill for 15 minutes on high. If you are using a charcoal grill, place an aluminum drip pan in the center of the firebox and build up the hot coals on both sides. If you are using a gas grill, set an aluminum drip pan on the grilling grate and place a rack inside the pan. Set another grilling grate 2 to 3 inches above the rack for the pork chops. Grill with the cover down.

2. Brush the chops with some melted lard and sprinkle with salt and pepper to taste. Grill, turning once and brushing with melted lard, for 10 minutes before placing the bread in the aluminum pan under the pork chops. Arrange the pieces of bread so they are directly under the chops and can collect the drippings. Grill, turning and basting occasionally, until golden brown and the ring of fat is slightly crisp, about another 30 minutes. If the bread starts to dry out

before enough drippings fall on them, brush lightly with melted lard. Remove the bread to a platter and place the chops on top. Sprinkle with more pepper and serve.

Makes 6 servings

Grilled Pork Chops Oregano

"Costolette di Maiale 'Riganatu'"

A simple Sicilian preparation that's very easy and deliciously flavored with the oregano and garlic in the marinade.

1 cup olive oil

4 garlic cloves, peeled and very finely chopped

1 onion, peeled and very finely chopped

$1/4$ cup very finely chopped fresh oregano

Salt and freshly ground black pepper

14 to 16 pork chops (about 2 pounds total), cut $1/4$ inch thick

1. Mix the olive oil, garlic, onion, oregano, and salt and pepper to taste in a 9 × 12-inch ceramic or glass baking pan. Dip both sides of the pork chops in this mixture and leave to marinate in the refrigerator, covered, for 4 hours, turning several times. Remove the pork chops from the refrigerator 15 minutes before grilling.

2. Prepare a medium-hot charcoal fire or preheat a gas grill for 15 minutes on medium-high.

3. Remove the pork chops from the marinade and discard the marinade. Place the pork chops with any marinade ingredients adhering to them on the grill. Cook, turning only once, until golden brown with black grid marks, about 10 minutes.

Makes 4 to 6 servings

Grilled Pork Chops Oregano; Grilled Stuffed Tomatoes from Sardinia (page 157)

Grilled Pork Chops with Juniper and Fennel Marinade

"Costòlette di Maiale alla Griglia"

Pork chops grilled with juniper and fennel was a favorite recipe of the great English food writer Elizabeth David. I've adapted her recipe but kept the chops rustic and succulent.

¹/₂ cup olive oil

1 tablespoon fennel seeds, ground

2 garlic cloves, peeled and finely chopped

10 dried juniper berries, ground

Salt and freshly ground black pepper

6 pork chops (about 2 ¹/₂ pounds total), cut 1 inch thick

1. Stir together the olive oil, fennel seeds, garlic, juniper berries, and salt and pepper to taste in a 9×12-inch ceramic or glass baking pan. Dip both sides of the pork chops in this mixture and then leave to marinate in the refrigerator, covered, for 4 hours, turning several times. Remove the pork chops from the refrigerator 15 minutes before grilling.

2. Prepare a hot charcoal fire or preheat a gas grill for 15 minutes on high.

3. Remove the pork chops from the marinade and place with any marinade ingredients adhering to them on the grill. Cook, turning only once, until golden with black grid marks, about 7 minutes on each side.

Makes 6 servings

It's Better at Room Temperature

Best results are attained when food is at room temperature before being grilled. But don't leave meat out of the refrigerator for longer than 15 minutes.

Tuscan-Style Spit-Roasted Pork Loin with Rosemary

"Àrista"

This roast pork loin, a traditional Sunday dish in Arezzo and Florence in Tuscany, can also be grilled instead of spit-roasted. The loin should be cut from the bone and weigh between 3 and 4 pounds.

The spit-roasted or grilled pork can also be eaten at room temperature. Twenty-four hours of marinating permeates the loin with flavor, while spit-roasting keeps the meat moist and succulent. This recipe is a favorite with guests and frees the host or hostess from lots of hands-on cooking. Don't forget to let the loin rest before carving, to let the juices settle.

Àrista is delightful with Grilled Portobello Mushrooms (page 163) and roast potatoes.

One 4-pound whole boneless pork loin, rib half, split open halfway (not all the way through) lengthwise

6 tablespoons finely chopped fresh parsley

6 garlic cloves, peeled and finely chopped

6 sprigs fresh rosemary

Freshly ground black pepper

1/4 pound pork fat, cut into thin strips or slices

1/2 cup olive oil

1 1/2 cups dry white wine

2 bay leaves, crumbled

Salt

1. Lay the pork loin in front of you with the split side up. Spread the parsley, garlic, and leaves from 2 rosemary sprigs down the center. Pepper to taste and close the loin up, holding it in place with toothpicks. Lay the slices of pork fat over the cut side along the length of the loin. Place the remaining sprigs of rosemary over the loin and tie tightly in three places with butcher's twine. Remove the toothpicks.

2. Place the loin in a 9 × 12-inch ceramic or glass baking pan and add the olive oil, white wine, and bay leaves. Leave to marinate in the refrigerator, covered, for 24 hours, turning several times. Remove the loin from the refrigerator 15 minutes before spit-roasting.

3. Prepare a medium-hot charcoal fire or preheat a gas grill for 15 minutes on medium. Set up the rotisserie attachment.

4. Remove the loin from the marinade and reserve the marinade. Secure the loin firmly to the spit, making sure the weight is evenly distributed so that the spit will rotate smoothly. Be sure the holding prongs on each end are tight and grip the loin solidly. If necessary, tie the loin to the spit with butcher's twine so it will not slide while the spit rotates. Salt and pepper to taste.

5. Place an aluminum drip pan on the grilling grate underneath the meat. Spit-roast until a meat thermometer registers an internal temperature of 175°F, about 2 hours. Baste every 15 minutes with some of the marinade mixed with pan juices collected in the drip pan. Remove the loin from the spit and let rest for 20 minutes before slicing. Carve into ⅜-inch-thick slices and serve.

Makes 6 to 8 servings

What's in a Name?

One explanation behind the name of *àrista* is that it originated during a banquet of the Ecumenical Council in Florence in 1430 when several Greek bishops exclaimed *aristos* ("the best" in Greek) when they ate this dish. Like all culinary-invention stories, this one seems fanciful. Giordano di Pisa had already used the word *àrista* in 1304 to describe a butcher's cut of pork back. In reality the etymology is unknown but thought to be pre-Indo-European.

Tuscan-Style Spit-Roasted Pork Loin with Rosemary; Grilled Portobello Mushrooms (page 163)

How to Roast a Pig

There are two ways in which this traditional roast suckling pig is prepared in Sardinia. The first method is to dig a large pit in the ground and line it with rocks. A large fire is built on the rocks, and when it has burned for many hours, the pig is placed on it and covered with hot coals. The pig is then covered with myrtle branches and the earth is piled on top so that there is no evidence of anything happening underground. This method was typical among the bandits who once populated the desolate reaches of the island's interior.

In the second method—the one I've chosen for this recipe—the Sardinian cook builds a fire from aromatic woods such as juniper, mastic, olive, arbutus, or holm-oak. The pig is affixed, head down, to a large, strong, preferably aromatic stake that will be stuck into the ground. A cross of two pieces of wood is tied to the bottom of the stake to keep the pig from slipping down, and the feet are splayed and tied to the ends of another cross on top of the stake. The fire is made and left to "blaze away merrily," as the Italian cookbook writer Ada Boni put it. Then the stake is driven into the ground about 20 inches in front of the fire and the pig is roasted chest side first. During roasting, it is basted with a hunk of pork fat or salt pork skewered onto a long fork or a two-pronged stick. Once the pig is done, it is smothered with myrtle leaves and left for 30 minutes before carving.

In place of the exotic woods, build a fire with whatever wood you have available. Once you begin to roast the pig, throw any combination of leftover nut shells, thyme, marjoram, oregano, mint, or basil twigs, bay leaves, olive briquets, or water-soaked apple wood chips onto the fire to create an aromatic smoke. When the pig is finished, you smother it with myrtle leaves. In this country myrtle is used only as an ornamental plant, and you are unlikely to find it pesticide-free. After experimenting, I believe that the closest concoction to approximate myrtle is a mixture of bay and sage leaves. If neither of these is available, use rosemary leaves.

If you lack an outdoor fireplace, you will have to dig a shallow fire pit. Choose an open area without overhanging branches or shrubs. Mark off a 3-foot-square area and dig down 6 inches. Remove any roots. Line and fill the hole with any nonporous igneous rocks you find lying around or with the lava rocks sold commercially as replacement rocks for gas grills. Now you are ready to build a fire.

Sardinian Roast Suckling Pig

"Porceddu"

This magnificent roast suckling pig from Sardinia requires a grand occasion—perhaps a wedding, a holiday, or a reunion of great friends. It is well worth the effort, an effort that also provides much fun.

One 15- to 18-pound suckling pig, cleaned

One 1-pound piece pork fat or salt pork

Aromatic leaves from bay, sage, and rosemary

1. Prepare a hardwood fire (see page 12) and let it burn for 3 hours, replenishing as needed with wood, until you have a good supply of hot coals. Affix the pig to a sturdy 4-foot-long wooden stake (see Box). Tie 2 crisscrossed sticks with twine a few inches from one end of the stake and 2 other crossed sticks about 10 inches from the end that will go into the ground. This might take you 15 minutes. Drive the stake into the ground up to 10 inches so that it doesn't tip over, placing it 20 inches in front of the fire, with the pig's chest toward the fire. The pig should be leaning slightly toward the fire. Make sure there is an aluminum drip pan in front of the pig. The pig will not fall over if the stake is deep enough.

2. Roast the pig, basting it with the salt pork or pork fat every 15 minutes, until the skin is cracking open, about 3 hours. Turn and continue to roast, basting every 15 minutes, until the meat near the shoulder can almost be pulled off with your fingers, about another 3 hours. Let the pig sit on a bed of the aromatic leaves for 30 minutes before carving.

Makes 15 servings

Grilled Beef Rolls with Bread and Pancetta

"Uccelletti di Campania"

The name of this popular Roman preparation means "little country birds," referring to how the rolled-up meat resembles skewered thrushes or other little birds. I love the delicious skewered meat, bread, and aromatic herb combination, and I believe you will too.

2 pounds flank steak

12 thin slices prosciutto (about
 $^{1}/_{3}$ pound)

12 fresh sage leaves

Freshly ground black pepper

Eight 10-inch wooden skewers

$^{1}/_{4}$ pound pancetta, sliced thinly

About $^{1}/_{4}$ loaf French or Italian
 bread, cut into twelve 1-inch
 cubes

Salt

Olive oil or melted lard for
 drizzling

1. Prepare a medium-hot charcoal fire or preheat a gas grill for 15 minutes on medium. If you are using a charcoal grill, you can, if you like, mound the coals to either side of an aluminum drip pan to collect the juices.

2. Butterfly the flank steak: lay it on a surface with a long side facing you. Using a long slicer or even a bread knife, slice the steak in half horizontally. Guide the blade through the meat by placing your hand flat on top of the meat but slightly behind or on top of where the blade is slicing to avoid accidentally cutting your hand. Slice carefully so the meat stays intact.

3. Cut the butterflied flank steak into twelve 3 × 5-inch slices. Place each slice of meat between 2 pieces of wax paper and flatten with a mallet or the side of a heavy cleaver until very thin, being careful not to tear the meat.

4. Lay a slice of prosciutto and 1 sage leaf on each slice of meat. Pepper to taste. Roll the meat up and form with your hands so the rolls stay shut and secure with a toothpick.

5. Double skewer all the ingredients: hold 2 skewers parallel to each other about $^1\!/_2$ inch apart between your thumb and forefinger. Skewer a steak roll-up, a slice of pancetta, and a cube of bread in that order until all the meat is skewered, placing 3 of each on each set of skewers. Salt to taste.

6. Drizzle some olive oil or lard over the skewers, place on the grill, and cook, turning occasionally, until golden, 25 to 30 minutes. If you used a drip pan, pour the collected juices over the "birds."

Makes 4 to 6 servings

Grilled Beef Rolls with Prosciutto and Mozzarella

"Involtini alla Paesana"

This popular meat roll-up from Sicily is double skewered, and each roll-up is stuffed with an exotic bread crumb, pine nut, and raisin stuffing. I like to serve the involtini *with Neopolitan-Style Tomato Salad (page 189).*

18 large bay leaves, preferably fresh

2 tablespoons golden raisins

1 ³/₄ pounds beef round or flank, butterflied (see preceding recipe, step 2) and cut into twelve 3 x 5-inch slices

1 small onion, peeled and finely chopped

1 cup bread crumbs, plus additional for coating

¹/₂ cup finely diced mozzarella

2 tablespoons pine nuts

1 slice prosciutto, ¹/₁₆ inch thick, finely chopped

1 large egg, beaten

Salt

Twelve 8- to 10-inch wooden skewers

Olive oil for drizzling

1. Prepare a hot charcoal fire or preheat a gas grill for 15 minutes on high.

2. If using dried bay leaves, soak them in tepid water for 30 minutes and drain. Soak the raisins in tepid water for 15 minutes.

3. Place the beef slices between 2 pieces of wax paper and flatten with a mallet or the side of a heavy cleaver until they are about ¹/₁₆ inch thick.

4. Mix together the onion, 1 cup of the bread crumbs, the mozzarella, pine nuts, and prosciutto. Drain the raisins and stir in. Place a heaping tablespoon of stuffing on each beef slice. (You can freeze any left-over stuffing for later use.) Carefully roll up the slices and secure with toothpicks.

5. Beat the egg with a pinch of salt and spread additional bread crumbs on a large plate. Dip the beef rolls into the egg and then the bread crumbs, making sure all surfaces are breaded.

6. Double skewer all the ingredients: hold 2 skewers parallel to each other about ½ inch apart between your thumb and forefinger. Skewer a bay leaf, then a beef roll, another bay leaf, another beef roll, and a bay leaf, putting 2 *involtini* and 3 bay leaves on each set of skewers.

7. Drizzle olive oil over the rolls and place on the grill for 7 minutes. Brush more olive oil over the rolls, turn, and grill until golden brown, about another 7 minutes.

Makes 4 to 6 servings

Hood Up or Down?

To maintain heat, it is best to keep the hood or cover down when grilling. This is especially important in cool weather. Every time you cover or uncover the grill, the cooking time changes, and you will be lifting or opening the hood or cover enough to baste, turn, or just look at the food.

Grilled Beef Rolls with Pecorino, Currants, and Pine Nuts

"Braciolettine Arrostite"

These beef involtini are popular fare in the summertime around Palermo in Sicily. The stuffing is a well-seasoned combination of currants, pine nuts, and pecorino cheese, typical Sicilian flavors of Arab influence. Serve with Grilled Vegetable Platter (page 165).

12 large bay leaves, preferably fresh

1 tablespoon currants

1 ³/₄ pounds beef round or flank, butterflied (see page 34, step 2) and cut into twelve 3 x 5-inch slices

2 tablespoons olive oil, plus additional for brushing

6 tablespoons bread crumbs

2 tablespoons freshly grated pecorino cheese

1 tablespoon pine nuts

6 tablespoons finely chopped onion

Salt and freshly ground black pepper

Twelve 8- to 10-inch wooden skewers

1 large onion, peeled, quartered, and separated

1. Prepare a hot charcoal fire or preheat a gas grill for 15 minutes on high.

2. If using dried bay leaves, soak them in tepid water for 30 minutes and drain. Soak the currants in tepid water for 15 minutes.

3. Place the beef slices between 2 pieces of wax paper and flatten with a mallet or the side of a heavy cleaver until they are about $1/16$ inch thick.

4. In a small frying pan, heat 2 tablespoons of the olive oil over medium-high heat. Add the bread crumbs and cook, stirring, until lightly browned, about 5 minutes. Remove the pan from the heat. Drain the currants and add to the bread crumbs with the pecorino, pine nuts, onion, and salt and pepper to taste. Mix thoroughly and set aside.

5. Brush each slice of beef with the additional olive oil and place a heaping tablespoon of stuffing on each beef slice. (You can freeze any leftover stuffing for later use.) Carefully roll up the slices and secure with toothpicks.

6. Double skewer all the ingredients: hold 2 skewers parallel to each other about $^1\!/_2$ inch apart between your thumb and forefinger. Slide a bay leaf, a piece of onion, and a beef roll onto each set of skewers in that order, using two of each ingredient for each set of double skewers.

7. Place the skewers on the grill close to the fire if possible and baste with olive oil. Cook until golden brown, 5 to 7 minutes on each side.

Makes 4 to 6 servings

Grilled T-Bone Steak from Florence

"Bistecca alla Fiorentina"

In the region around Florence, a tall, lean, and heavy breed of cattle called Chianina is raised: a two-year-old might weigh 2,000 pounds. But it is the steer between 14 and 16 months old that is used for this famous Florentine steak. Because we Americans have both very good beef and a tradition of grilling steaks, this famous preparation is easily replicated.

One 2 ³/₄-pound whole T-bone or Porterhouse steak (preferably "prime" quality), 1 ¹/₂ inches thick

Salt and freshly coarsely crushed black pepper

Extra-virgin olive oil for brushing

1. Prepare a hot charcoal or hardwood fire or preheat a gas grill for 15 minutes on high.

2. Sprinkle the steak with salt and pepper to taste and brush it lightly with olive oil. Carefully lay the steak on the gas grill or about 5 inches from a very hot fire. Do not move or touch the steak for 10 minutes. Turn, using a grill spatula or tongs. Grill until one side has black grid marks, about another 10 minutes, and remove from the fire to a serving platter. Salt and pepper to taste and brush both sides with olive oil. Serve. This is the amount of time for a rare steak.

Makes 4 servings

Steak at Its Best

Even given the simplicity of grilling a steak, there are a few things you should keep in mind for perfection. First, beef of "prime" quality is very expensive but worth the price in this special preparation. Do not pound, puncture, or otherwise "tenderize" a prime steak. It is called prime because it does not need tenderizing as it is raised to be tender. This is true for many USDA choice steaks, too.

A prime-quality steak should be cooked very rare, rare, or medium-rare. If you like your steak more done, you should use a less expensive quality such as "choice." Or use a different cut entirely, such as London broil, although then you would be getting away from the whole point behind a Florentine steak.

Breaded Grilled Sirloin Steak, Palermo Style

"Bistecca 'Mpanata' alla Palermitana"

The next two recipes from Palermo originally disguised the taste of poor-quality meat, but in the United States, with our high-quality beef, they just make good meat even more delightful.

1 bay leaf

1 1/2 cups bread crumbs

Salt and freshly ground black pepper

6 sirloin steaks (about 3 3/4 pounds total)

1/4 cup olive oil spread on a large plate

1. Prepare a hot charcoal fire or preheat a gas grill for 15 minutes on high.

2. Crumble the bay leaf into the bread crumbs, add salt and pepper to taste, and spread on a large plate. Dip the steaks in the olive oil and then dredge in the bread crumbs, patting the steaks to coat them thoroughly.

3. Place the steaks on the grill and cook, turning only once, to desired doneness.

Makes 6 to 8 servings

Breaded Grilled Sirloin Steak, Palermo Style; Grilled Onions (page 167)

Marinated and Breaded Sirloin Steak, Grilled Sicilian Style

"Bistecca 'Mpanata' alla Griglia"

In this recipe the steaks are marinated for about 12 hours before they are breaded and grilled. The flavor is somewhat richer than that of the preceding recipe.

1 cup olive oil, plus additional for drizzling

1/2 cup red wine vinegar

2 garlic cloves, peeled and finely chopped

2 tablespoons finely chopped fresh basil

Freshly ground black pepper

6 sirloin steaks (about 3 3/4 pounds total)

1 1/2 cups bread crumbs

1/2 cup freshly grated parmesan cheese

1 tablespoon dried oregano

Salt

1. Mix together 1 cup of the olive oil, the vinegar, garlic, basil, and pepper to taste in a 9 × 12-inch ceramic or glass baking pan. Dip both sides of the steaks in this mixture and then leave to marinate in the refrigerator, covered, for 12 hours, turning several times. Remove the steaks from the refrigerator 15 minutes before grilling.

2. Prepare a hot charcoal fire or preheat a gas grill for 15 minutes on high.

3. Remove the steaks from the marinade and discard the marinade. Spread the bread crumbs on a large plate and mix in the parmesan and oregano. Salt the steaks to taste and dredge in the bread crumbs, patting the steaks to coat them thoroughly. Drizzle with a little olive oil. Place the steaks on the grill and cook, turning only once, to desired doneness.

Makes 6 to 8 servings

The Telling Touch

When testing for doneness, don't cut open with a knife; learn to tell doneness by touch. Undercook food so that you still have the option of throwing it back on the grill. Overcooked food is irretrievable. Because fires differ, I recommend you look at and feel the food rather than relying exclusively on suggested cooking times.

Sicilian-Style Grilled Skewered Meatballs

"Spiedini"

This Sicilian recipe is an example of cucina arabo-sicula, *Sicilian cuisine influenced by the medieval Arab era. The Arab influence is evident in the molding of the ground meat around the skewer.*

1 pound ground beef, ground twice (ask the butcher to do this or use a meat grinder or food processor)

1 large egg, beaten

$^{1}/_{2}$ cup freshly grated pecorino cheese

$^{1}/_{2}$ cup bread crumbs

2 tablespoons finely chopped fresh parsley

1 garlic clove, peeled and finely chopped

Salt and freshly ground black pepper

About $^{1}/_{2}$ loaf French or Italian bread, cut into eighteen 1-inch cubes

2 ounces pancetta, sliced $^{1}/_{16}$ inch thick, cut into 1-inch squares

Twelve 8- to 10-inch wooden skewers

Olive oil for basting or drizzling

1. In a medium-size mixing bowl, knead the ground beef, egg, pecorino, bread crumbs, parsley, garlic, and salt and pepper to taste. Form the meat into 18 walnut-sized balls. Leave the meat to rest in the refrigerator, covered, for 30 minutes.

2. Prepare a medium-hot charcoal fire or preheat a gas grill for 15 minutes on medium.

3. Double skewer all the ingredients: hold 2 skewers parallel to each other about $^{1}/_{2}$ inch apart between your thumb and forefinger. Skewer the meatballs, bread cubes, and pancetta in that order, placing no more than 3 of each ingredient on a double skewer.

4. Place the skewers on the grill and cook, turning occasionally and basting with olive oil, until the meat and bread are golden brown, 15 to 20 minutes. Drizzle with olive oil after being grilled if desired.

Makes 4 servings

Sicilian-Style Grilled Skewered Meatballs

Calabrian-Style Grilled Skewered Meatballs

"Spiedini"

In Calabria, the toe of the Italian boot, when they say spiedini, *they mean these rustic skewers of grilled ground beef flavored with salami, parsley, and sage.*

1 cup fresh bread crumbs

¹/₂ cup milk

1 pound ground beef, ground twice (see Note)

1 large egg

3 tablespoons freshly grated pecorino cheese

1 tablespoon lard, softened at room temperature

¹/₄ pound salami, peeled (if necessary) and finely chopped

2 tablespoons finely chopped fresh parsley

24 slices pork fat back, ¹/₁₆ inch thick, cut into ³/₄-inch squares

24 fresh sage leaves

About ¹/₂ loaf Italian or French bread, cut into twenty-four 1-inch cubes

Sixteen 10-inch wooden skewers

Olive oil or melted lard for basting

1. Prepare a medium-hot charcoal fire or preheat a gas grill for 15 minutes on medium.

2. Soak the bread crumbs in the milk and then squeeze the milk out. Place the soaked bread crumbs in a medium-size mixing bowl. Mix and knead the crumbs with the meat, egg, pecorino, lard, salami, and parsley. Form the meat into 24 walnut-sized balls and set aside.

3. Double skewer all the ingredients: hold 2 skewers parallel to each other about ¹/₂ inch apart between your thumb and forefinger. Skewer the meatballs, fat, sage leaves, and bread cubes in that order, placing no more than 3 of each ingredient on a double skewer.

4. Place the skewers on the grill and cook, turning frequently, until golden brown, about 20 minutes. Baste frequently with the olive oil or melted lard during grilling. Discard the fat after grilling.

Makes 4 to 6 servings

Note: Ask the butcher to do this or use a meat grinder or food processor.

Grilled Beef As You Like It

For grilling beef, the fire should be hot enough so that you are not able to hold the palm of your hand 3 inches over the fire for more than one second. A 1-inch-thick steak is medium rare when poking the steak with your index finger feels identical to poking the flesh of your palm just below your thumb. A $^3/_4$-inch-thick sirloin steak takes 5 minutes per side on a high gas fire or 4 to 5 inches over a charcoal fire for very rare.

I never grill prime beef more done than medium rare—you just lose flavor that way. If you like your steaks well done, use less expensive, tougher cuts of meat such as blade steak or London broil, which benefit from longer cooking times. Cooking a tender steak, such as filet mignon, until well done simply toughens it, defeating the purpose of buying a tender steak in the first place.

Grilled Steak Sandwich with Pesto

This purely American invention makes good use of Italian inspiration for a great sandwich. The iceberg lettuce is used for its crunchy texture, and the pesto makes up for what the lettuce lacks in taste.

$1/2$ cup Pesto (page 196)

1 $1/4$ pounds sirloin tip, sliced
   into 2- to 3-inch pieces

Salt and freshly ground black
   pepper

Olive oil for dipping

6 soft rolls, 5 inches in diameter
   or 8 inches in length; or
   1 Italian loaf cut crosswise
   into 5-inch-long pieces

12 leaves iceberg lettuce

1 large ripe tomato, sliced very
   thinly

1 small red onion, peeled and
   sliced very thinly

1. Prepare a hot charcoal fire or preheat a gas grill for 15 minutes on high.

2. Prepare the pesto.

3. Place the sirloin pieces between 2 sheets of wax paper and flatten with a mallet or the side of a heavy cleaver until quite thin. Cut into approximately 5×3-inch pieces. Salt and pepper to taste and dip in olive oil.

4. Place the meat slices on the grill and cook until they change color, 2 to 3 minutes on each side.

5. Slice open the rolls and spread the pesto on both sides. Layer the lettuce, steak, tomato, and red onion and serve.

Makes 6 servings

Grilled Steak Sandwich with Pesto

Grilled Veal Rolls with Pine Nuts and Raisins

"Involtini de Vitello"

Veal roll-ups are very popular in Sicily. During the last century, there wasn't much meat in Sicily, and what there was, was of poor quality. So cooks came up with ingenious ways of making a little meat go a long way, such as flattening the meat and stuffing it. In this preparation the veal is pounded very thin and stuffed with bread crumbs and an aromatic mixture of golden raisins, cheese, pine nuts, and salami.

$1/2$ cup golden raisins

18 large bay leaves

2 pounds veal scallopine, cut into twelve 3 x 5-inch slices, $1/8$ to $1/4$ inch thick

$1/4$ cup olive oil, plus additional for drizzling and brushing

1 small onion, finely chopped

2 cups bread crumbs

$1/2$ cup grated caciocavallo or pecorino cheese

$1/3$ cup pine nuts

8 very thin slices soppressata or other salami, cut into small bits

1 plum tomato, peeled, seeded, and finely chopped

1. Prepare a medium-hot charcoal fire or preheat a gas grill for 15 minutes on medium-high.

2. Soak the raisins in tepid water for 15 minutes and then drain. Soak the bay leaves in tepid water until needed; drain.

3. Place the pieces of veal scallopine between 2 pieces of wax paper and flatten with a mallet or the side of a cleaver until they are about $1/16$ inch thick.

4. In a medium-size frying pan, heat 2 tablespoons of the olive oil over medium heat. Add the chopped onion and cook, stirring, until translucent, 7 to 8 minutes. Add 1 cup of the bread crumbs and 2 more tablespoons of the oil and cook, mixing thoroughly, for 1 to 2 minutes. Remove the pan from the heat. Add the cheese, raisins, pine nuts, soppressata, tomato, and salt and pepper to taste and mix again.

Salt and freshly ground black pepper

2 large eggs, beaten

1 medium-size onion, peeled, quartered, and separated

Twelve 8- to 10-inch wooden skewers

5. Place a heaping tablespoon of stuffing on each veal slice and carefully roll up. Secure with toothpicks. Dip the veal rolls into the beaten eggs and then the remaining bread crumbs, making sure all surfaces are breaded.

6. Double skewer all the ingredients: hold 2 skewers parallel to each other about ½ inch apart between your thumb and forefinger. Skewer a bay leaf, a piece of onion, and a veal roll. Repeat, then end with a bay leaf.

7. Drizzle olive oil over the rolls and place on the grill for 8 to 10 minutes. Brush with more olive oil, turn, and grill on the other side, brushing with olive oil, until golden brown, 8 to 10 more minutes.

Makes 6 servings

Let Your Senses Be Your Guide

The cooking times in the recipes should be used with caution because fires differ so dramatically in heat, depending on many factors, such as the size of the grill, whether the hood is up or down, how many coals have been used, and how cold it is outside. It is best to use the times as guides, always resting your final judgment about doneness on the look, touch, and smell of the food.

Grilled Veal Rolls with Mortadella and Pecorino

"Braciolettine Arrostite alla Messinese"

*T*his involtini *is a simpler version of the previous one, but just as good. Remember that the key to these roll-ups is to grill them slowly and baste frequently.*

¹/₂ cup bread crumbs

2 tablespoons finely chopped fresh parsley

2 garlic cloves, peeled and very finely chopped

¹/₃ cup freshly grated pecorino cheese

Freshly ground black pepper

Olive oil

1 ¹/₄ pounds veal scaloppine, cut into eight 3 x 5-inch slices, ¹/₈ to ¹/₄ inch thick

8 thin slices unsalted butter (about 3 tablespoons)

8 slices mortadella

Salt

Eight 8- to 10-inch wooden skewers

Melted lard or butter for basting

1. Prepare a medium-hot charcoal fire or preheat a gas grill for 15 minutes on medium-high.

2. Mix together the bread crumbs, parsley, garlic, pecorino, and pepper to taste. Add enough olive oil to make a paste.

3. Place the pieces of veal between 2 pieces of wax paper and flatten with a mallet or the side of a heavy cleaver until they are about ¹/₁₆ inch thick.

4. Place a thin slice of butter on every rectangle of meat, then cover with a slice of mortadella, trimming to the same size if necessary. Cover the mortadella with some of the bread crumb mixture and lightly sprinkle with salt. Roll up and secure with toothpicks.

5. Double skewer the roll-ups: hold 2 skewers parallel to each other about ¹/₂ inch apart between your thumb and forefinger. Slide the roll-ups onto the skewers so they fit tightly, using 2 roll-ups per double skewer.

6. Place the skewers on the grill and cook until golden brown, 8 to 10 minutes on each side. Baste frequently with the melted lard or butter.

Makes 4 servings

Grilled Veal Rolls with Pancetta

"Involtini alla Griglia"

This preparation is also simple but has that highly rustic flavor coming from the pancetta. It is stuffed with garlic and parsley–flavored bread crumbs and grilled with a basting of lard.

$3/4$ cup bread crumbs

3 tablespoons freshly grated pecorino cheese

1 garlic clove, peeled and finely chopped

2 tablespoons finely chopped fresh parsley

Freshly ground black pepper

1 pound boneless veal leg or loin, cut into eight $2^1/_2$ x $2^1/_2$-inch slices

Salt

Olive oil

$1/4$ pound pancetta, sliced thinly

Eight 8- to 10-inch wooden skewers

Melted lard for basting

1. Prepare a hot charcoal fire or preheat a gas grill for 15 minutes on high.

2. In a medium-size mixing bowl, mix together the bread crumbs, pecorino, garlic, parsley, and pepper to taste.

3. Place each slice of veal between 2 sheets of wax paper and flatten with a mallet or the side of a heavy cleaver until thin and about 4 × 3 inches.

4. Place a heaping tablespoonful of stuffing on one end of the veal slice and roll up, folding the side edges in. Mold with your hands or secure with a toothpick. Salt to taste. Pour some olive oil into a large plate and dip the veal slices in the oil.

5. Double skewer all the ingredients: hold 2 skewers parallel to each other about $1/2$ inch apart between your thumb and forefinger. Skewer a piece of pancetta, then a veal roll. Repeat, then end with pancetta.

6. Place the skewers on the grill and cook, basting with the melted lard, until golden brown, 8 to 10 minutes on each side.

Makes 4 servings

Grilled Veal Rolls with Mozzarella and Prosciutto

"Involtini allo Spiedo"

It is a delight to cut into these scrumptious rolls of grilled veal with their oozing mozzarella. The scallopine should be pounded quite thin before it is stuffed with mozzarella and prosciutto. Do not salt anything because the pancetta has enough salt for the whole dish.

1 pound boneless veal shoulder or loin, cut into 10 to 12 slices

10 to 12 slices prosciutto (about 3 to 4 ounces)

$1/4$ pound fresh mozzarella cheese, cut into 10 to 12 slices

Freshly ground black pepper

About $1/4$ pound pancetta, cut into 6 thick slices, and cut in half

Four 10-inch wooden skewers

Olive oil for basting

1. Prepare a medium-hot charcoal fire or preheat a gas grill for 15 minutes on medium-high.

2. Place each veal slice between 2 pieces of wax paper and flatten with a mallet or the side of a heavy cleaver until it is $1/16$ inch thick and at least 5×3 inches. Cover each slice of veal with a slice of prosciutto and a piece of mozzarella. Pepper to taste.

3. Roll up, press closed with your hands, and secure the ends with a toothpick so the cheese will not ooze out during grilling.

4. Double skewer all the ingredients: hold 2 skewers parallel to each other about $1/2$ inch apart between your thumb and forefinger. Put 5 to 6 roll-ups interspersed with pieces of pancetta on each set of double skewers.

5. Place the skewers on the grill and cook, turning occasionally, until golden brown, about 20 minutes. Baste frequently with olive oil.

Makes 4 servings

Grilled Veal Rolls with Mozzarella and Prosciutto; Grilled Artichokes (page 158)

Grilled Veal Chops

"Costolette di Vitello alla Griglia"

There is no need to get overly fancy when grilling a high-quality veal chop. The tenderness of the veal will carry the day. Spaghetti with only black or red pepper, a drizzle of olive oil, and a little parmesan cheese is the perfect accompaniment. As with all chops and steaks, these grill best over a very hot hardwood fire.

6 tablespoons olive oil

6 tablespoons red wine

2 sprigs fresh rosemary, leaves chopped

Freshly ground black pepper

6 veal loin chops (about 3 pounds total)

Salt

Lemon wedges

1. Mix the olive oil, red wine, rosemary, and pepper to taste in a 9×12-inch ceramic or glass baking pan. Dip both sides of the veal chops in this mixture and then leave to marinate in the refrigerator, covered, for 2 hours, turning several times. Remove the veal chops from the refrigerator 15 minutes before grilling.

2. Prepare a very hot hardwood or charcoal fire or preheat a gas grill for 15 minutes on high.

3. Drain the veal chops. Salt them, place on the grill, and cook until golden with black grid marks, 4 to 5 minutes on each side. Garnish with the lemon wedges.

Makes 6 servings

Variation: Replace the red wine with either white wine or balsamic vinegar.

Spit-Roasted Leg of Lamb, Aretina Style

"Arrosto d'Agnello all'Aretina"

Grilled lamb marinated in olive oil and vinegar and studded with rosemary, a method from Arezzo in Tuscany, is a fine combination on the grill. The wafting aroma will make your guests huddle, drooling, around the grill.

One 4-pound boneless leg of
  lamb, rolled and tied with
  twine (buy it this way or ask
  the butcher)

4 garlic cloves, peeled, 3 finely
  chopped, 1 slivered

2 teaspoons chopped fresh
  rosemary

3/4 cup olive oil

3/4 cup dry white wine

1/4 cup red wine vinegar

Juice of 1 lemon

1 tablespoon dried oregano

1 bay leaf, crumbled

Salt and freshly ground black
  pepper

1. Make several incisions in the lamb and stuff them with slivers of garlic and rosemary.

2. Stir together the olive oil, white wine, wine vinegar, lemon juice, oregano, bay leaf, and salt and pepper to taste in a large deep ceramic or glass bowl or casserole. Place the lamb in the bowl and leave to marinate in the refrigerator, covered, for 6 hours, turning several times. Remove the lamb from the refrigerator 15 minutes before grilling.

3. Prepare a hot charcoal fire or preheat a gas grill for 15 minutes on high. Set up the rotisserie attachment.

4. Secure the lamb firmly to the spit, making sure the weight is evenly distributed so the spit rotates smoothly. Make sure the holding prongs on each end are tight and grip the lamb solidly. If necessary, tie the lamb to the spit with butcher's twine so it will not slide while the spit rotates. Spit-roast, basting with the marinade every 10 minutes, until the surface is brown and crusty, about 2 hours. Remove the lamb from the fire and spit and let rest for at least 15 minutes before carving.

Makes 6 to 8 servings

Spit-Roasted Whole Leg of Lamb

"Agnello allo Spiedo"

The secret to this simple spit-roasted leg of lamb is to keep the fire fueled with aromatic woods and herbs. Whether you are making a hardwood or charcoal fire or using a gas grill, the smoke will provide the basic flavor. Try rosemary, oregano, or thyme twigs; apple wood chips; olive briquets; or almond, hazelnut, or chestnut shells. Soak whichever aromatics you choose in water before adding to the fire (except, of course, the olive briquets).

One 11- to 12-pound whole leg of lamb

Salt and freshly ground black pepper

Cayenne pepper (optional)

Olive oil for brushing

A brush made of fresh oregano and thyme sprigs

1. Prepare a medium-low charcoal fire or preheat a gas grill for 15 minutes on medium-low. Add rosemary, thyme, or other herb twigs (soaked first for 10 minutes in water) to the charcoal fire or to the aromatic wood chip container of a gas grill (see pages 5–8 for a description of alternatives). The lamb will spit-roast for 4 hours, so you will need to replenish the fire periodically with more herbs or apple chips, hazelnut or almond shells, or other woods. Set up the rotisserie attachment.

2. Season the leg of lamb with salt and pepper to taste and, if desired, cayenne, and brush with olive oil.

3. Secure the lamb firmly to the spit, making sure the weight is evenly distributed so the spit rotates smoothly. Make sure the holding prongs on each end are tight and grip the lamb solidly. If necessary, tie the lamb to the spit with butcher's twine so it will not

Spit-Roasted Whole Leg of Lamb; Grilled Red, Yellow, and Green Peppers (page 156)

slide while the spit rotates. Spit-roast, basting with the herb brush dipped in olive oil every 20 minutes, until the meat feels tender enough to pull off the bone with your fingers, about 4 hours. Remove the lamb from the fire and spit and let it rest 20 to 30 minutes before carving.

Makes 8 servings

Rest the Roast

After grilling, let larger pieces of grilled or spit-roasted meats rest at least 10 to 15 minutes before serving so the juices can settle (usually this will happen without planning for it).

Thin Lamb Chops Marinated in Wine and Herbs

"Bracioline d'Agnello alla Brace"

In its simplest version braciolino, *a thin chop, lamb in this case, is splashed with olive oil, sprinkled with salt and pepper, and grilled to perfection. This recipe marinates the lamb for a long time, making it tender and flavorful.*

Don't grill the lamb chops too close to the fire. If you have an adjustable grilling grate, raise it; if you don't have an adjustable grate, build the fire to one side of the grill or cook on medium with a gas grill.

It may seem easier in step 3 to baste the lamb with the marinade than to handle the hot lamb, but by dunking the lamb in the marinade, the meat is not merely brushed but soaked.

6 lamb chops (2 ½ pounds total), cut ½ inch thick

¼ cup olive oil

5 garlic cloves, peeled and finely chopped

¾ cup dry white wine

1 tablespoon dried oregano

1 tablespoon finely chopped fresh sage

1 tablespoon finely chopped fresh rosemary leaves

Juice of 1 lemon

Salt and freshly ground black pepper

A brush made of fresh rosemary sprigs

1. Coat the lamb with the olive oil and all the remaining ingredients except the rosemary brush in a 9×12-inch ceramic or glass baking pan. Marinate in the refrigerator, covered, for 6 to 8 hours, turning several times. Remove the lamb from the refrigerator 15 minutes before grilling.

2. Prepare a medium-hot charcoal fire or preheat a gas grill for 15 minutes on medium.

3. Remove the lamb from the marinade and reserve the marinade. Place the lamb on the grill and baste with the marinade, using the rosemary brush. Cook without turning for 15 to 20 minutes. Remove the lamb from the grill and dip it in the marinade. Replace on the grill on its other side until medium-rare and springy to the touch, another 15 to 20 minutes.

Makes 5 to 6 servings

Variation: Add chopped onions to the marinade.

Grilled Lamb Rib Chops

"Scottadito"

This Roman favorite is the height of simplicity, and its name, scottadito, *literally means "burnt fingers," which gives you an idea about how to eat the rib chops. Cut off the fat and pieces of meat from the rib bone so you have a nice "handle," saving the scraps for another use. You'll need to gently pound the rib eye until it is a bit thinner.*

12 lamb rib chops (about 2 $\frac{1}{2}$ pounds total)

Salt and freshly ground black pepper

$\frac{1}{4}$ cup melted lard

1. Prepare a hot charcoal fire or preheat a gas grill for 15 minutes on high.

2. Trim the lamb chops and flatten slightly with a mallet. Salt and pepper to taste. Brush with melted lard and place on the grill. Cook, basting with more melted lard, until golden brown, 8 or 9 minutes on each side.

Makes 4 servings

The Virtues of Patience

Once the food is on the grill, be patient and don't fiddle with it. Don't keep turning the food unless the recipe instructs you to do so. Every time you squeeze or poke food on the grill, you lose precious juices, especially from meats, and the opportunity to develop attractive grid marks. Never use two-pronged forks with anything being grilled.

Grilled Skewered Kid with Lemon and Onion Marinade

"Spiedini di Capretto alla Molisana"

In the Molise province of Italy, kid is grilled on skewers with pieces of pork fat, turned a few times, and seasoned only with salt and pepper. Further south, in Apulia, kid is grilled with oil, vinegar, and oregano. In this recipe you can omit the skewers if you want and replace the kid with lamb.

¹/₄ cup olive oil

Juice of 1 lemon

1 small onion, peeled and finely chopped

3 tablespoons finely chopped fresh parsley

Salt and freshly ground black pepper

1 ¹/₂ pounds boneless kid or lamb chops, cut into chunks if using skewers

Six 10-inch wooden skewers (optional)

1. Mix together the olive oil, lemon juice, onion, parsley, and salt and pepper to taste in a 9 × 12-inch ceramic or glass baking pan. Add the meat, turn to coat with the mixture, and leave to marinate in the refrigerator, covered, for 2 hours, turning a few times. Remove the meat from the refrigerator 15 minutes before grilling.

2. Prepare a hot charcoal fire or preheat a gas grill for 15 minutes on high.

3. Remove the meat from the marinade, reserving the marinade. Skewer the meat if using skewers. Place the meat on the grill and cook, turning once, until golden brown, 8 to 10 minutes on each side. Baste twice with the marinade.

Makes 4 servings

3

Sausages, Variety Meats, and Mixed Meats

Homemade Italian Sausage on the Grill

"Salsiccia Fresca"

This is the classic Sicilian recipe for sausage, the basis of which is sold throughout the United States as Italian sausage. The recipe yields 8 pounds of sausage. For 4 to 6 servings, set aside about 2 pounds of sausage. Divide the remaining sausage into 3 large zipper plastic freezer bags for future use.

6 pounds boneless pork shoulder, with its fat, coarsely chopped or ground

2 pounds pork fat back, coarsely chopped or ground

6 tablespoons fennel seeds

1/4 cup salt

2 tablespoons freshly ground black pepper

1 1/2 cups freshly grated pecorino cheese

1 tablespoon red pepper flakes (optional)

1 cup dry white wine

25 feet hog (sausage) casing

1. In a large mixing bowl, mix the pork shoulder, pork fat, fennel seeds, salt, black pepper, pecorino, red pepper flakes if using, and wine. Refrigerate, covered, 4 hours or overnight.

2. Open one end of the hog casing and slip it over the water faucet. Turn the water on gently to wash out the casing. Then slide one end of the casing over the funnel of the sausage-stuffing attachment of a meat grinder or mixer. Push all of the casing you are using onto the length of the funnel (it will contract and fit fine), leaving about 2 inches dangling from the end. Tie this end in a double knot.

3. Turn the grinder on and begin to add the cold marinated pork mixture. As the ground pork begins to push into the casing, it will push the casing off the funnel. Have a large bowl or platter at hand to catch the sausages. Twist to make links or leave to make one continuous sausage. Do not overstuff the casing or it will burst now or later during cooking. Be careful that the sausage stuffing enters the casing continuously and that no air bubbles develop. If air bubbles

do develop, it is better to cut the sausage at that point and start a new sausage by tying an end off. Or you can prick the air bubbles with a skewer.

4. Prepare a low charcoal fire or preheat a gas grill on low for 15 minutes.

5. Place the sausages in a large pot and cover with water. Bring to a boil over high, and just as the water begins to bubble, reduce the heat to low so the water doesn't boil and poach the sausages for 10 minutes.

6. Drain the sausages and place them on the grill. Cook the sausages, turning them frequently, until brown and no longer mushy to the touch, about 45 minutes.

Makes 8 pounds sausage

Making Sausage

Because pigs are raised quite lean today, it is necessary to add pork fat in order to make a truly wonderful-tasting sausage. Sausages are made with a 3 to 1 ratio of meat to fat. If you reduce the fat, your sausage will be dry and crumbly.

Hog, or sausage, casings can be bought from supermarket butchers or any butcher that makes sausages. They are already cleaned, and all you need to do is rinse away the preserving salts. Make sure all the ingredients, especially the meat, are very cold, including the grinder blade of the meat grinder. This prevents the meat and fat from smearing together and looking like pâté. Obviously, you will need some specialized equipment: a meat grinder or mixer with sausage-stuffing attachment.

Grilled Homemade Beef and Lamb Sausages, Apulia Style

"Zambitta"

Zambitta *are sausages from Apulia made with fatty beef or veal and lamb meat. In this preparation the sausage is formed into one long link that is coiled and secured with long metal skewers, then grilled. If the meat you use is very lean, you must add about 2 pounds of mixed beef and lamb fat.*

This recipe yields 6 pounds of sausage. For 4 to 6 servings, set aside 2 pounds of sausage. Divide the remaining sausage into 2 large zipper plastic freezer bags for future use.

2 ¹/₂ pounds coarsely chopped or ground beef (not more than 75% lean)

2 ¹/₂ pounds coarsely chopped or ground lamb (not more than 75% lean)

1 pound chopped lamb or beef fat (ask the butcher)

1 cup freshly grated pecorino cheese

¹/₄ cup finely chopped fresh basil

¹/₄ cup finely chopped fresh parsley

3 tablespoons salt

2 tablespoons freshly ground black pepper

1. Prepare all the ingredients (except the casing) into sausage meat and seasonings, and stuff the casing, according to the instructions on pages 68–69, without marinating and without twisting into links.

2. Arrange the sausage in one long spiral and skewer with 20-inch metal skewers in 3 places to hold together.

3. Prepare a low charcoal fire or preheat a gas grill on low for 15 minutes.

4. Place the sausage spiral on the grill. Cook, turning it frequently with hot pads, until brown and no longer mushy to the touch, 30 to 40 minutes.

Makes 6 pounds

3 tablespoons fennel seeds

25 feet hog (sausage) casing

Three 20-inch metal skewers

Note: This sausage is not parboiled, usually an essential treatment to prevent bursting; therefore both sausage and fire require some attention during grilling to prevent flare-ups, hot spots, and bursting.

Sausage Savers

Grill sausages over a low to medium gas fire or over the cool spot of a charcoal grill. Grill them slowly, without flames, because of the possibility of flare-ups. Turn frequently. Although it's an extra step, parboiling sausages briefly before grilling is essential to keep them from bursting as a result of the intense heat of a grill.

Grilled Skewers of Sausage, Orange, and Bay Leaf

"Spiedini di Salsiccia e Arancio"

Fresh, juicy oranges skewered and grilled with sausage are an unusual but quite refreshing summertime treat. The bay leaf and onion provide an enticing aroma as you grill. Discard the bay leaf but plan to eat all of the orange, including the peel.

10 bay leaves

1 ¹/₂ medium-size onions, cut into wedges

6 links Italian sweet sausage, homemade (page 68) or commercial, cut into equal-sized chunks

1 Florida juice orange, with peel, cut into chunks the same size as the sausage

Ten 8- to 10-inch wooden skewers; or 5 metal skewers

Olive oil for drizzling

1. Soak the bay leaves in tepid water for 30 minutes while you work so they soften; drain.

2. Prepare a medium-hot charcoal fire or preheat a gas grill for 15 minutes on medium-high.

3. Double skewer all the ingredients: hold 2 skewers parallel to each other about ¹/₂ inch apart between your thumb and forefinger. Skewer a piece of onion, then a bay leaf, a piece of sausage, and a piece of orange, repeating that order until all the ingredients are used up. There should be 2 or 3 pieces of meat per double skewer.

4. Coat each skewer with a drizzle of olive oil and place on the grill. Cook, turning occasionally, until the sausage is browned and the oranges slightly blackened on the edges, about 20 minutes.

Serves 2 or 3

Grilled Skewers of Sausage, Orange, and Bay Leaf; saffron orzo

Mixed Grill

"Misto Griglia"

You may want to use a different combination than I suggest below, such as veal kidney, lamb leg, and T-bone, or perhaps skirt steak, duck breast, and veal chop.

1 ¼ pounds beef rib-eye
  steaks, about 1 inch thick

1 ¼ pounds veal chops, about
  1 inch thick

1 ¼ pounds lamb chops, about
  1 inch thick

Olive oil

Salt and freshly ground black
  pepper

1. Prepare a hot charcoal fire or preheat a gas grill for 15 minutes on high.

2. Dip all the meats in a 9 × 12-inch ceramic or glass baking pan filled with olive oil, coating them on both sides. Salt and pepper generously.

3. Carefully place the rib-eye steaks, veal chops, and lamb chops on the grill and do not touch or move them; turn only once. The veal chops grill for 12 minutes, the lamb chops grill for 10 minutes, and the rib-eye grills 8 minutes for rare.

4. Remove the meat from the grill and transfer to a large serving platter. Salt and pepper to taste and serve.

Makes 6 to 8 servings

Mixed Grill, Italian Style

Mixed grills are popular throughout Italy. Typically, the cook chooses three or more types of meat to grill over a blazing lump hardwood charcoal fire and serves them with grilled vegetables (see Grilled Vegetable Platter, page 165).

Because of the sheer simplicity of a mixed grill, you will want to do two things to make sure that the finished product is something to remember: first, have three or more types of meat, and second, once the meat is placed on the grill, do not touch or poke it until it is time to turn, then turn only once.

Woodcutter's-Style Mixed Grill

"Misto Griglia degli Boscaioli"

This mixed grill is an example of the range of possibilities when it comes to mixing meats and vegetables to be grilled. This preparation is a popular one with guests because there is so much variety of taste and texture on each skewer.

$^1/_2$ **polenta recipe (page 168)**

Six 10-inch wooden skewers

$^3/_4$ **pound Italian sausages, homemade (page 68) or commercial, cut into 12 pieces**

12 button mushrooms (about $^1/_2$ pound), stems removed

1 pound pork cutlets, cut into 12 pieces

3 tablespoons finely chopped fresh rosemary leaves

Salt and freshly ground black pepper

Olive oil for drizzling

1. Prepare the polenta through step 5 on page 169. Cut into twelve 1-inch cubes.

2. Prepare a hot charcoal fire or preheat a gas grill for 15 minutes on high.

3. Skewer 2 pieces of sausage, 2 mushrooms, 2 pieces of pork, and 2 polenta cubes onto each skewer, in that order. Sprinkle with rosemary, add salt and pepper to taste, and drizzle with olive oil.

4. Place the skewers on the grill and cook, turning occasionally, until the meat is golden brown, the mushrooms dark brown, and the polenta is slightly blackened, 15 to 17 minutes.

Makes 6 servings

Woodcutter's-Style Mixed Grill; grilled zucchini

Grilled Rabbit and Sausage Skewers, Molise Style

"Coniglio alla Molisana"

There are all kinds of recipes in Italy for rabbit, wild rabbit, and hare. In Sicily, they grill wild rabbits with a marinade of olive oil, garlic, vinegar, and oregano. In central Italy, hare is spit-roasted with olive oil and flavored with bay leaves, parsley, and cloves. Sometimes the grilled hare is served with a sauce made from the liver and blood of the hare and chopped onions, stock, wine, and lemon juice.

In Sondrio, Lombardy, a preparation called lepre con la crostada *is a spit-roasted hare that is then stewed in cream and crushed macaroons. Calabrians like to marinate hare in vinegar and scallions overnight and then skewer the meat with pancetta and bay leaves before grilling.*

Several handfuls of fresh or dried rosemary, oregano, and marjoram twigs

1 rabbit (about 3 pounds)

4 links Italian sausage (about 1 pound total), homemade (page 68) or commercial, cut into 1-inch pieces

1 tablespoon finely chopped fresh parsley

1 tablespoon finely chopped fresh rosemary

Salt and freshly ground black pepper

1. Prepare a low charcoal fire or preheat a gas grill for 15 minutes on low. Toss several handfuls of mixed dried or fresh herb twigs onto the fire. (See pages 5–8 for instructions for gas grills.)

2. Because there is not an abundance of meat on a rabbit, slice the meat very close to the bone, using both a boning and paring knife and trying to keep the pieces as large as possible. (Save the bones for the rabbit stock used in Pappardelle with Rabbit Sauce, page 184.) Put the rabbit and sausage pieces in a mixing bowl and toss with the parsley, rosemary, and salt and pepper to taste.

3. Lay a piece of rabbit on a section of a paper-thin prosciutto slice and roll up. Skewer the rolled-up rabbit with a sage leaf and a sausage piece, in that order, until all the ingredients are used up.

12 paper-thin slices prosciutto (about ¼ pound total)

12 large fresh sage leaves

Four 10-inch wooden skewers

Olive oil for basting

4. Place the skewers on the grill and cook, turning occasionally, until golden brown, about 1 hour. Baste with olive oil during grilling.

Makes 4 servings

Variation: Alternatively, instead of rolling the rabbit pieces in prosciutto, cut the prosciutto into ⅛-inch-thick squares of 1 inch and skewer with the rabbit and the sausage.

Grilled Turkey Scallopine Stuffed with Sausage

"Involtini di Tacchino e Salsiccia"

The sausages are juicy enough to keep the turkey-scallopine wrapping moist through the grilling. These involtini *are great with a simple salad.*

5 to 6 link Italian sausages, (about 1 pound), homemade (page 68) or commercial

1 pound boneless, skinless turkey breast, cut into 5 or 6 scallopine slices (or buy it already sliced)

Freshly ground black pepper

20 fresh sage leaves

Six 8- to 10-inch wooden skewers

Olive oil

1. Prepare a medium-hot charcoal fire or preheat a gas grill for 15 minutes on medium.

2. Place the sausages in a large pot and cover with water. Bring to a boil, and just as the water begins to bubble, reduce the heat to below a boil and poach the sausages for 10 minutes. Drain and set aside.

3. Place each slice of turkey between 2 pieces of wax paper and flatten with a mallet or the side of a heavy cleaver until it is about 3 × 5 inches, being careful not to break through the flesh. Lightly salt and pepper each slice of turkey, place a sausage link at one end, and roll up, securing with a toothpick.

4. Double skewer all the ingredients: hold 2 skewers parallel to each other about ½ inch apart between your thumb and forefinger. Skewer 1 or 2 sage leaves, then a roll-up, another 1 or 2 sage leaves, another roll-up, and more sage leaves.

5. Pour olive oil into a large plate, dip the roll-ups in the oil, and add salt and pepper to taste. Place the skewers on the grill and cook, basting with any remaining olive oil, until golden brown, about 15 minutes on each side.

Makes 4 servings

Grilled Turkey Scallopine Stuffed with Sausage; Neapolitan-Style Tomato Salad (page 189); roasted potatoes

Lombard-Style Mixed Grill

"Misto Griglia del Longobardo"

This mixed grill from Milan is popular because everyone loves the variety of flavors, ranging from polenta and red bell peppers to sausages and tenderloin.

1/2 polenta recipe (page 168)

10 ounces beef tenderloin, cubed

10 ounces pork tenderloin, cubed

10 ounces veal liver, cubed

10 ounces Italian sausages (about 3 links), homemade (page 68) or commercial, sliced into 1-inch rounds

32 to 40 large fresh sage leaves

1 to 2 red bell peppers, cored, seeded, and cut into 1-inch squares

Salt and freshly ground black pepper

Olive oil for drizzling

Eight 10-inch wooden skewers

For the horseradish sauce:

3/4 cup freshly grated horse-radish (about 2 ounces)

1/2 teaspoon salt

1 teaspoon sugar

1/2 cup whipped cream

1. Prepare the polenta recipe through step 5 on page 169. Cool and cut into the same cube shapes as the meat.

2. Prepare a medium-hot charcoal fire or preheat a gas grill for 15 minutes on medium.

3. Skewer all the ingredients in any order you wish. Place the skewers on the grill and cook, turning occasionally, until the beef and pork are golden brown, about 20 minutes.

4. Meanwhile, whip the horseradish, salt, sugar, and whipped cream together and serve with the mixed grill.

Makes 4 servings

Apulia-Style Rustic Sausages

"Gniummeriddi"

This kind of preparation—grilling variety meats and herbs wrapped in caul fat—is popular all over rural southern Italy, but it is especially popular in Apulia, in the region of Gargano, where they grill it over olive wood.

I find that most Americans have not developed a taste for mixed grilled variety meats—even though they are fantastically delicious—and so I include this recipe for those who would like to experiment. You will not be disappointed in this new experience.

$1/2$ **pound pork caul fat (page 16), cut into 5 x 7-inch rectangles**

$3/4$ **pound lamb or veal heart, cut into $3/4$-inch cubes**

$3/4$ **pound lamb or veal liver, cut into $3/4$-inch cubes**

$3/4$ **pound lamb or veal kidney, cut into $3/4$-inch cubes**

24 fresh sage leaves

$1/4$ **pound pecorino crotonese cheese (page 17) or provolone cheese, cut into strips about 3 inches long**

$1/4$ **pound pork or lamb fat, cut into strips about 3 inches long**

24 sprigs fresh parsley

Salt and freshly ground black pepper

Lemon wedges

1. Prepare a low charcoal fire or preheat a gas grill for 15 minutes on low.

2. Carefully (because it's fragile) unravel and spread the caul fat on a surface. If you are unable to get 5×7-inch rectangles, use a patchwork of caul fat. Skewer 1 cube each of the heart, liver, and kidney, in that order, placing a sage leaf between the cubes (about 3 sage leaves per skewer). Lay the skewer on a rectangle of caul fat. Place a strip of pecorino, a strip of pork or lamb fat, and 2 to 3 sprigs of parsley on top, add salt and pepper to taste, and roll up tightly. The caul fat should adhere without problem, and the wrapped skewer will look like a thick sausage. Continue in this manner until all the ingredients are used to make 8 skewers.

3. Place the skewers on the grill and cook, turning frequently, until the caul fat is dark brown and the meat no longer squishy to the touch, about 45 minutes. Serve with lemon wedges.

Makes 8 skewers; 6 to 8 servings

Tuscan-Style Grilled Liver in Caul Fat

"Fegatelli alla Toscana"

This Tuscan recipe for grilled liver will please all but the most finicky eaters. The liver is wrapped in caul fat, which acts as a self-baster, so that you needn't even hang around minding the grill.

1 pound pork (preferred) or veal liver, cut into 1-inch cubes

1 cup bread crumbs

$^1/_2$ teaspoon fennel seeds

Salt and freshly ground black pepper

$^1/_4$ pound pork caul fat (page 16), cut into 5-inch squares

Six 8-inch wooden skewers

About $^1/_4$ loaf Italian or French bread, cut into twelve 1-inch cubes

12 bay leaves, soaked in tepid water 30 minutes and drained

1. Prepare a low charcoal fire or preheat a gas grill for 15 minutes on low.

2. Toss the liver cubes with the bread crumbs, fennel seeds, and salt and pepper to taste.

3. Carefully (because it's fragile) unravel and spread the caul fat on a surface. If you are unable to get 5-inch squares, use a patchwork of caul fat. Place several chunks of liver on each section of caul fat and roll up, wrapping the caul fat into tight little packages. You should have 12 little packages.

4. Skewer a liver package, a bread cube, and a bay leaf, in that order, until all the ingredients are used up. Use 2 liver packages, 2 bread cubes, and 2 bay leaves per skewer.

5. Place the skewers on the grill and cook, turning occasionally, until the caul fat is golden brown and springy, not mushy, to the touch, about 25 minutes.

Makes 4 servings

Variation 1: Marinate the liver for 1 hour in the juice of 1 lemon, 3 finely chopped sage leaves, and leaves from 1 sprig of rosemary; omit the bread crumbs and fennel seeds.

Variation 2: Add 3 ounces of pecorino crotonese cheese (a semisoft eating pecorino) or provolone cheese, sliced into thin strips, to the liver packages.

Variation 3: In Sicily the liver chunks are studded with small pieces of provola cheese and parsley, wrapped in caul, and skewered with onion sections and bay leaves before they are grilled.

Ya Gotta Have Pluck

Sardinians are famed for their rustic grilled variety meats, such as the *cordula* made by shepherds. *Cordula* is a braided grilled sausage casing with chunks of heart and liver seasoned with sage, dried juniper berries, thyme, marjoram, salt, and pepper. Another Sardinian preparation, called *ortau,* is casings stuffed with pig's blood, fried lard, liver, tongue, heart, spleen, and lung, all chopped very fine with parsley and garlic. *Trattalia* is a typical farmhouse preparation of grilled pluck (the heart, liver, and lungs) and reticulum (the second stomach of a ruminant animal) with bay leaves and roasted bread cubes. The *trattalia* is wrapped in aromatic leaves such as grape leaves or myrtle. It is cooked in a trench lined with stones, where a fire is built with mixed woods. This style of cooking is called *a carrargiu* in Sardinian dialect.

In Sicily a preparation similar to *Gniummeriddi* (Apulia-Style Rustic Sausages, page 83) called *stigghiole* is a street food sold by special vendors called *'u stigghiularu,* or *stigghiole* sellers. The aroma is very enticing as you pass by.

Grilled Heart of Beef

"Cuore di Bue sulla Brace"

Beef heart is a good introduction to grilled variety meats because the flavor is not at all unusual—it tastes like beef. This recipe includes oregano, garlic, and olive oil and works very well with veal kidneys also.

1 ³/₄ pounds beef heart (see Note), sliced ¹/₄ inch thick

¹/₄ cup olive oil

Salt and freshly ground black pepper

1 teaspoon dried rosemary or oregano

2 garlic cloves, peeled and finely chopped

Juice of 1 lemon

1. Arrange the sliced heart in a 9×12-inch ceramic or glass baking pan and coat with the olive oil, salt and pepper to taste, rosemary or oregano, garlic, and lemon juice. Toss well. Leave to marinate in the refrigerator, covered, for 2 hours, stirring once or twice. Remove the heart from the refrigerator 15 minutes before grilling.

2. Prepare a low charcoal fire or preheat a gas grill for 15 minutes on low.

3. Remove the heart from the marinade, reserving the marinade. Place the sliced heart on the grill and cook, turning occasionally, until golden brown, about 20 minutes. Baste with the marinade during grilling.

Makes 4 servings

Note: Ask the butcher at your supermarket to order beef or veal heart.

4

Poultry and Game Birds

Grilled Chicken Marinated in Onions and Garlic

"Pollo Marinato alla Griglia"

The secret to a luscious golden-brown grilled chicken, especially if it has its skin on, is to grill slowly. Do not use a cover because flare-ups will occur. These marinated chickens will be a lovely golden color after about 30 minutes of grilling.

Two 3-pound free-range chickens, quartered

1 cup olive oil

$^1/_4$ cup finely chopped fresh parsley

2 onions, peeled and thinly sliced

3 garlic cloves, peeled and finely chopped

Salt and freshly ground black pepper

1. Place the chicken pieces in a large ceramic or glass baking pan and cover with the olive oil, parsley, onions, garlic, and salt and pepper to taste. Leave to marinate in the refrigerator, covered, for 4 hours, turning occasionally. Remove the chicken from the refrigerator 15 minutes before grilling.

2. Prepare a medium-hot charcoal fire or preheat a gas grill for 15 minutes on low. For charcoal grills, the grilling grate should be 12 inches from the source of the heat if adjustable; otherwise, mound the coals to one side and grill the chicken over the cool spot with an aluminum drip pan underneath to catch the drippings. If using a gas grill, place a rack on the grill with the drip pan underneath. Keep the pan filled with water as the chicken grills. If you cook without a rack, directly on the grill, watch for flare-ups.

3. Remove the chicken from the marinade and reserve the marinade. Place the chicken on the grill, uncovered, and cook, basting with the marinade, until golden, 20 to 30 minutes on each side.

Makes 6 servings

Grilled Chicken

"Pollo alla Griglia"

Perfectly grilled chicken has no black burn marks nor any black film from flare-ups. It should have a crisp, golden skin and lusciously moist meat that melts in your mouth. To achieve this, follow the recipe.

6 chicken legs (about 3 1/2 pounds total)

Olive oil for coating

Salt and freshly ground black pepper

1. Prepare a medium-hot charcoal fire or preheat a gas grill for 15 minutes on low. For charcoal grills, the grilling grate should be 12 inches from the source of the heat if adjustable; otherwise, mound the coals to one side and grill the chicken over the cool spot with an aluminum drip pan underneath to catch the drippings. If using a gas grill, place a rack on the grill with the drip pan underneath. Keep the pan filled with water as the chicken grills. If you cook without a rack, directly on the grill, watch for flare-ups.

2. Coat the chicken with olive oil and salt and pepper to taste. Place the chicken legs on the grill and cook, turning occasionally, until golden brown, about 1 hour 45 minutes.

Makes 4 to 6 servings

Note: If you are unable to raise the chicken 12 inches from the heat source, the cooking time will be shorter. Do not let the fat from the chicken drip on the fire.

Making it Crispy

Chicken and duck with skin should be grilled farther from the coals or in the cool spot of the grill, covering, uncovering, and moving the pieces as needed to prevent flare-ups. Place an aluminum drip pan filled with some water underneath the chicken or duck, with the coals on either side of the pan, so that the fat will drip into it. When cooking chicken and duck, you want to be careful not to grill it too quickly; otherwise, the skin will blacken before the inside is cooked instead of becoming crispy.

Grilled Chicken Oregano

"Pollo Origanato"

This Sicilian recipe is a quick way to grill chicken, and the results are an utterly delectable mélange of garlic, oregano, and lemon juice. If you decide to use boneless, skinless chicken breasts, they will cook even faster than boneless thighs. Serve with Grilled Eggplant Roll-Ups (page 161).

½ cup olive oil

3 tablespoons freshly squeezed lemon juice

2 garlic cloves, peeled and very finely chopped

2 tablespoons finely chopped fresh parsley

1 tablespoon dried oregano

Salt and freshly ground black pepper

2 pounds boneless, skinless chicken thighs

1. Prepare a hot charcoal fire or preheat a gas grill for 15 minutes on high.

2. Mix together the olive oil, lemon juice, garlic, parsley, oregano, and salt and pepper to taste in a 9 × 12-inch ceramic or glass baking pan. Dip the chicken pieces in this mixture.

3. Remove the chicken from the marinade and reserve the marinade. Place the chicken on the grill and cook, basting often with the marinade, until springy to the touch, about 10 minutes on each side.

Makes 4 servings

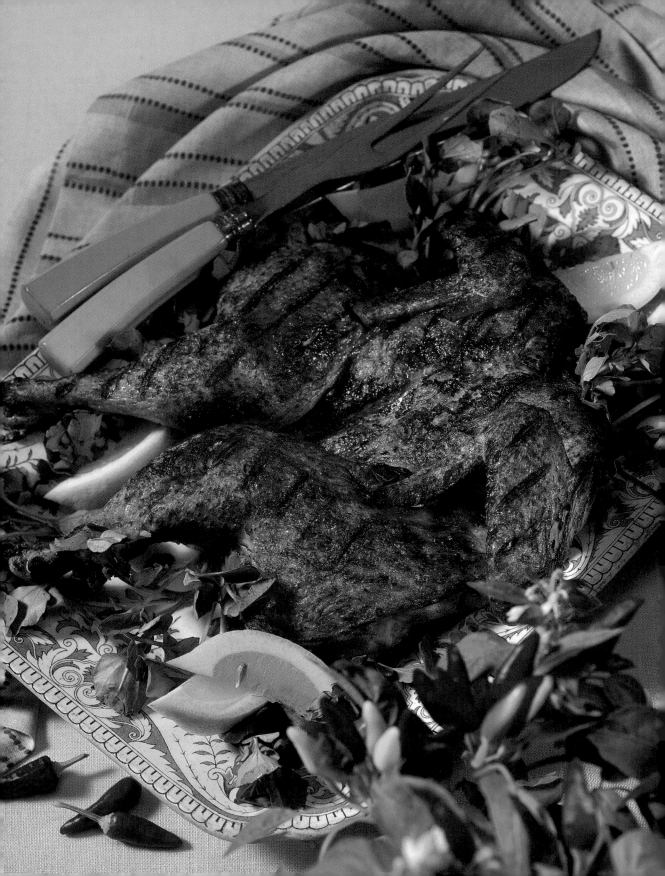

The Devil's Chicken

"Pollo alla Diavolo"

The name of this recipe, said to have originated in Rome, is applied to two very different methods. In Rome and Florence, cooks like to coat the chicken with olive oil, lemon juice, and lots of pepper before grilling; hence the name alla diavolo, *or hot as the devil. In southern Italy the chicken is marinated in white wine and sage and then grilled and served salted and peppered.*

In either case, the common technique is to split the chicken open down the middle of the back, spread it out, and flatten it by heavy pounding on the breast with the side of a cleaver or a mallet. The chicken must be basted constantly with butter or olive oil so that it doesn't dry out. When finished, it has an appetizing golden-brown sheen.

It is best to use pullet or cockerel, a plump, very young free-range or semi-free-range chicken. In older recipes the chicken is marinated in olive oil, onion, parsley, salt, pepper, and ground ginger for 4 hours and served with lemon and watercress. You could also replace the chicken with 4 Cornish hens or 6 pigeons.

One 4-pound young chicken, split down the backbone and pounded very flat, without breaking bones

¹/₂ cup olive oil

Salt

Cayenne pepper

Lemon wedges

1. Place the chicken in a large and deep ceramic or glass baking pan or enameled casserole and add the olive oil, salt, and plenty of cayenne pepper. Leave to marinate in the refrigerator, covered, for 2 hours. Turn every 15 minutes. Remove the chicken from the refrigerator 15 minutes before grilling.

2. Prepare a medium-hot charcoal fire or preheat a gas grill for 15 minutes on medium. For charcoal grills, the grilling grate should be 12 inches from the source of the heat if adjustable; otherwise, mound the coals to one side and grill the chicken over the cool spot with an aluminum drip pan underneath to catch the

drippings. If using a gas grill, place a rack on the grill with the drip pan underneath. Keep the pan filled with water as the chicken grills. If you cook without a rack, directly on the grill, watch for flare-ups.

3. Remove the chicken from the marinade and reserve the marinade. Lay the chicken on the grill and cook, turning occasionally and basting every once in a while with the marinade, until golden brown, about 45 minutes. Serve garnished with the lemon wedges.

Makes 4 servings

Variation 1: Make a marinade of ½ cup olive oil, 1 small onion, peeled and finely chopped, 3 tablespoons finely chopped fresh parsley, 1 teaspoon ground ginger, and some salt and pepper to taste. Marinate the chicken for 6 hours.

Variation 2: Coat the chicken with olive oil, some freshly squeezed lemon juice, salt, and lots of pepper and grill for 45 minutes, basting with more olive oil or melted butter.

Variation 3: Place the chicken in a large ceramic or glass baking pan and cover with 1 cup white wine, 3 tablespoons finely chopped fresh sage, 2 tablespoons olive oil, salt, and lots of pepper. Marinate for 6 hours, turning occasionally.

Devilish Ways

About thirty years ago I ate *pollo alla diavolo* in a trattoria in Florence. I asked how it was cooked, and the waiter, who must have learned English in England, said that the chicken was spatchcocked and then grilled. I didn't know what the word meant and had to look it up later. It comes from an eighteenth-century Irish expression that means any "dispatched cock," a fowl split open and grilled after being summarily killed (dispatched).

Grilled Stuffed Chicken Breasts

"Petti di Pollo Ripieno alla Griglia"

This delightful recipe is an involtini, *a flattened chicken scallopine stuffed with a mixture of fresh bread, nutmeg, garlic, and mortadella, and wrapped in pancetta. It's delicious with Grilled Polenta (page 168).*

4 boneless, skinless chicken breast halves (1 to 1 1/4 pounds total)

Salt and freshly ground black pepper

About 1/2 loaf Italian or French bread, white part only, ripped into small pieces (about 3 cups)

3 ounces mortadella, chopped

Pinch of grated nutmeg

2 tablespoons finely chopped fresh parsley

1 large garlic clove, peeled and finely chopped

2 large eggs, lightly beaten

1/4 pound pancetta, thinly sliced

Olive oil for drizzling

1. Prepare a medium-hot charcoal fire or preheat a gas grill for 15 minutes on medium-high.

2. Place the chicken breasts between 2 pieces of wax paper and flatten with a mallet or the side of a heavy cleaver until they are about 3 × 5-inch scallopine. Salt and pepper the chicken breasts to taste.

3. Prepare the stuffing by kneading the bread, mortadella, nutmeg, parsley, garlic, and eggs together in a mixing bowl. Divide the stuffing into quarters, place each quarter of stuffing on one end of a flattened breast, and roll up. Wrap the breasts in pancetta, securing the pancetta and the ends of the roll-ups with toothpicks.

4. Drizzle the roll-ups with olive oil, place on the grill, and cook, turning occasionally, until golden brown, about 20 minutes.

Makes 4 servings

Grilled Free-Range Chicken Breasts

"Petti di Pollo sulla Graticola"

A free-range chicken is so naturally good-tasting that all it needs is a simple grilling. The chicken that ranges freely to feed is superior to a factory-grown chicken, and you may have to ask the butcher specially for it. A grilled free-range chicken hardly needs an accompanying sauce, but you could try any of the sauces in chapter 8 or the lemon sauce in the Variation below.

4 free-range boneless, skinless chicken breast halves (1 $\frac{1}{4}$ to 1 $\frac{1}{2}$ pounds total)

Salt and freshly ground black pepper

Olive oil for drizzling

1. Prepare a hot charcoal fire or preheat a gas grill for 15 minutes on high.

2. Split the breast halves if they are still attached to each other, add salt and pepper to taste, and drizzle with olive oil.

3. Place the chicken on the grill and cook, turning only once, until golden brown, about 7 minutes on each side.

Makes 4 servings

Variation: This grilled chicken can stand alone, or you could try a tart lemon sauce. Melt 2 tablespoons butter in a small pan, pour in the juice and grated zest from 1 lemon, and and add $\frac{1}{2}$ teaspoon sugar. Season with salt and pepper. Cook over medium-high heat until the sauce reduces by half and pour over the chicken or serve on the side.

Keeping Lean Meats Juicy

Lean meats, such as rabbit and chicken breast, should be grilled close to the very hot coals to sear the meat quickly and trap all the juices. To accomplish this with fixed grilling racks, keep the coals mounded instead of spreading them out.

Spit-Roasted Cornish Hens

"Gallina allo Spiedo"

Slow spit-roasting produces a memorable chicken. The flavors of sage, rosemary, pancetta, and garlic enhance this already perfect taste. This recipe calls for Cornish hens instead of chicken because they make terrific individual servings. It also works well with quail.

4 Cornish hens (about 1 1/2 to 1 3/4 pounds each)

1/2 cup olive oil

2 tablespoons finely chopped fresh sage

4 large sage leaves

2 sprigs fresh rosemary, leaves finely chopped

1/4 pound pancetta, half chopped, half thinly sliced

2 garlic cloves, peeled and chopped

A brush made of 4 fresh rosemary sprigs

1. Placethe hens in a 9×12-inch ceramic or glass baking pan, add the olive oil, and then sprinkle with half the sage and half the chopped rosemary. Leave to marinate in the refrigerator, covered, for 3 hours, turning occasionally. Remove the hens from the refrigerator 15 minutes before grilling.

2. Prepare a low charcoal fire or preheat a gas grill for 15 minutes on medium-low. For charcoal grills, the grilling grate should be 12 inches from the source of the heat if adjustable; otherwise, mound the coals to one side and grill the chicken over the cool spot with an aluminum drip pan underneath to catch the drippings. If using a gas grill, place a rack on the grill with the drip pan underneath. Keep the pan filled with water as the chicken grills. If you cook without a rack, directly on the grill, watch for flare-ups. Set up the rotisserie attachment.

3. Mix the chopped pancetta with the garlic and remaining sage and chopped rosemary. Remove the hens from the marinade, reserving the marinade. Stuff the hens with the pancetta mixture. Lay a slice of pancetta over each hen. Truss the hens, making sure the twine secures the pancetta slices.

4. Secure the birds firmly to the spit, making sure their weight is evenly distributed so the spit rotates smoothly. Make sure the holding prongs on each end are tight and grip the hens solidly. If necessary, tie the hens to the spit with butcher's twine so they will not slide while the spit rotates. Grill until golden brown, about 1¼ to 1¾ hours. You can check for doneness by puncturing the inside of a leg with a skewer. If the juice is clear, the hens are done; if it's pink, continue cooking. Baste the hens by brushing with the rosemary sprigs dipped in marinade.

Makes 4 servings

Variation 1: Chop 3 ounces of prosciutto, 1 garlic clove, and 6 fresh sage leaves together. Mix together with ½ teaspoon fennel seeds and salt and pepper to taste. Stuff the body cavities of the Cornish hens with this mixture. Rub the skin all over with a crushed garlic clove. Drizzle olive oil all over the Cornish hens. Cover the hens with 3 ounces of thinly sliced fatty prosciutto. Put 1 crushed garlic clove and 3 ounces of chopped prosciutto in the craw and truss. Affix the hens securely to the spit and spit-roast for 1¼ to 1¾ hours.

Variation 2: Add rosemary to the stuffing mixture.

Spit-Roasted Cornish Hens; pappardelle with wild mushrooms

Spit-Roasted Cornish Hens with Juniper and Bay

"'Toresani' allo Spiedo"

Toresan *and* terraiuolo *are Venetian words for a certain kind of small pigeon known as squab. Because of the difficulty finding squab, not to mention the expense, I recommend using Cornish hens or young chickens.*

¼ cup olive oil

10 dried juniper berries, crushed

2 bay leaves, crumbled

Salt and freshly ground black pepper

4 sprigs fresh rosemary

4 Cornish hens or 2 young chickens (about 7 ½ pounds total)

2 ounces thinly sliced pancetta (4 to 8 slices)

---

1. Prepare a medium-low charcoal fire or preheat a gas grill for 15 minutes on medium-low. If using a charcoal grill, mound the coals to either side of the firebox and place an aluminum drip pan in the center. If using a gas grill, place a rack on the grill with an aluminum drip pan underneath. Set up the rotisserie attachment.

2. Mix the basting oil by stirring together the olive oil, juniper berries, bay leaves, and salt and pepper to taste.

3. Put a sprig of rosemary inside each hen or chicken. With a brush, dab some basting oil on the inside of the birds. Truss the birds. Wrap 1 or 2 pieces of pancetta around each. Tie the birds in two places, around the wings and around the breast, so the pancetta will not fall off and the birds are compact.

4. Secure the birds firmly to the spit, making sure their weight is evenly distributed so the spit rotates smoothly. Make sure the holding prongs on each end are tight and grip the birds solidly. If necessary, tie the birds to the spit with butcher's twine so they will not

slide while the spit rotates. Spit-roast, basting fairly often with the basting oil, until golden brown and moist, about 2 hours. Once you run out of the basting oil, baste with the collected pan juices.

Makes 6 servings

Grilled Turkey Steaks with Pomegranate Sauce

"Tacchina Arrostita alla Melagrana"

In Venetian this preparation is called paeta arosto col malgaragno, *roasted turkey with pomegranates. It's a dish typical of the countryside around Arzignano and Montebello, where a baby turkey is spit-roasted. In my recipe I've taken the basic concept and made it a little more manageable.*

2 pomegranates

¹/₄ pound pork caul fat (page 16)

3 tablespoons unsalted butter

1 tablespoon olive oil

¹/₄ cup very finely chopped onion

1 teaspoon finely chopped fresh sage

Salt and freshly ground black pepper

1. Hit the pomegranates lightly with a mallet or rolling pin, rolling them around on a counter. This will loosen and lightly crush the seeds inside. Make a small cut in the skin and pour the juice out into a bowl, squeezing to get as much juice out as possible. Remove the seeds from the pomegranates and set aside. Each pomegranate will yield a little more than a ¹/₂ cup of juice.

2. Chop 1 ounce (about the size of a walnut when the caul fat is rolled into a ball) of the caul fat very finely and set aside. Melt 1 tablespoon butter with the olive oil in a small saucepan over medium heat. Add the onion, sage, and chopped caul fat and cook, stirring occasionally, until the onion is translucent,

1 1/2 pounds boneless, skinless turkey breast, sliced into 4 steaks

8 leaves fresh mint for garnishing

about 8 minutes. Salt and pepper to taste. Pour in two-thirds of the reserved pomegranate juice, saving the remaining third to baste the turkey. Cook over medium heat until the juice thickens, about 5 minutes. Strain the sauce through a food mill or strainer, pushing with the back of a wooden spoon. Return the sauce to the pan and keep warm.

3. Prepare a low charcoal fire or preheat a gas grill for 15 minutes on low.

4. Melt the remaining butter and dip each turkey steak in it. Salt and pepper the turkey. Carefully (because it's fragile) unravel a piece of caul fat and lay it on a large plate. Place a turkey steak on one edge of the caul fat, cut the caul fat to fit around the turkey, and wrap the turkey up. Repeat for the rest of the turkey steaks.

5. Place the turkey on the grill. If your turkey steaks are cut from the thickest part of the breast and form an oval-shaped package about 2 inches thick, grill them, turning occasionally and basting with the remaining pomegranate juice, until golden brown, about 40 minutes. If your steaks are thinner, like chicken breasts, grill them, turning only once, for 6 to 8 minutes on each side over high heat or close to the fire. Transfer the turkey to a serving platter, pour the pomegranate sauce over, sprinkle with some of the reserved pomegranate seeds, and serve with a few leaves of fresh mint.

Makes 4 servings

Grilled Turkey Steaks with Pomegranate Sauce; potato cake

Spit-Roasted Duck, Sardinian Style

"Anitra Arrosto"

This bread crumb–coated spit-roasted duck becomes a gorgeous golden brown. The rich taste of duck is best accompanied by a simple salad and fresh crusty bread.

One 4 1/2- to 5-pound duck

2 tablespoons melted lard

Salt and freshly ground black pepper

1 cup bread crumbs

1. Prepare a medium-hot charcoal fire or preheat a gas grill for 15 minutes on medium. If using a charcoal grill, mound the coals to either side of the firebox and place an aluminum drip pan in the center. If using a gas grill, place a rack on the grill with an aluminum drip pan underneath. Set up the rotisserie attachment.

2. Dry the duck inside and out with paper towels. Save the innards for another use. Brush half the lard on the inside of the duck and salt and pepper to taste. Truss the duck. Secure the duck firmly to the spit, making sure the weight is evenly distributed so the spit rotates smoothly. Make sure the holding prongs on each end are tight and grip the duck solidly. If necessary, tie the duck to the spit with butcher's twine so it will not slide while the spit rotates.

3. Spit-roast the duck, basting at first with the remaining lard. As the duck turns, prick it all over with a skewer or corncob holders to let the fat run out. Once there is enough fat in the drip pan, use the duck fat for basting. After the duck has spit-roasted for 1 hour, remove the spit from the rotisserie with the duck still affixed. While resting the spitted duck over a large tray, salt lightly and coat with bread crumbs, pressing them onto the skin all over the duck. Refit

the spitted duck to the rotisserie and continue spit-roasting, without basting, until the bread crumbs are deep golden brown and crusty, about 45 minutes.

Makes 4 servings

Variation: Use 12 quail instead of the duck and separate them with bay leaves on the spit.

Grilled Quail

"Quaglia Arrosto"

As one food writer said, the Italians will shoot anything that flies and eat it. In the Veneto region, especially in Vicenza, they make polenta e osei, *songbirds, such as larks, thrushes, warblers, buntings, or blackbirds, and squares of polenta spit-roasted over a fire of aromatic woods. Osei is the Venetian dialect word for* uccelli, *small wild birds. You can use quail, squab, or Cornish hens in this recipe.*

12 quail

12 fresh sage leaves

Freshly ground black pepper

12 thin slices pancetta
    (about ¼ pound)

1. Prepare a medium-hot charcoal fire or preheat a gas grill for 15 minutes on medium.

2. Open the cavity of each quail and stuff with a sage leaf and a pinch of black pepper. Wrap a slice of pancetta around the breasts of each quail, securing it with a sturdy toothpick stuck directly through the body.

3. Place the quail on the grill and cook, turning occasionally, until golden brown on all sides, about 35 minutes.

Makes 6 servings

Variation: Add rosemary to the stuffing. Or for the Venetian dish *polenta e osei,* affix the birds to the spit securely, interspersed with sage leaves and polenta squares.

Grilled Quail; Grilled Polenta (page 168)

A Taste for Birds

The Italians are quite fond of grilling a great variety of game birds, songbirds, and waterfowl. Woodcock stuffed with bay leaf, juniper berries, and lard is spit-roasted and served on roasted bread with a pâté of chopped giblets. Snipe is stuffed with chopped goose liver, truffles, and spices, marinated in Marsala with ham, mushrooms, thyme, and lemon, then spit-roasted and served on toast with a sauce made from the marinade. Small birds such as thrush are wrapped in caul fat or vine leaves and spit-roasted. Aquatic birds like coot and rail are also grilled, as well as pigeons and squab.

5

Fish and Shellfish

Grilled Whole Fish

"Pesce alla Griglia"

There are only two things to keep in mind for perfect grilled fish: the fish must be very, very fresh, and you must attend the fish at all times. About half the weight of a whole fish is made up of inedible parts, that is, head, tail, bones, and viscera, so take that into account when deciding how much to buy. Generally, you can assume that 1 pound of whole fish will feed one person. Grilling a 3- to 6-pound fish is much easier with a hinged fish grill.

One 2 1/2- to 6-pound whole fish (Box, pages 134 to 135), scaled, gutted, cleaned, and patted dry with paper towels

1/4 cup olive oil

2 tablespoons finely chopped fresh parsley

Salt and freshly ground black pepper

1. Prepare a hot charcoal fire or preheat a gas grill for 15 minutes on high.

2. Dip both sides of the fish in a mixture of olive oil and parsley. Salt and pepper to taste.

3. Place the fish on the grill and cook, turning once, until most of the skin is blackened on both sides, the eyes are completely white, and the fish no longer mushy to the touch, about 10 minutes per inch thickness of fish measured at the thickest part. You can also check doneness by pulling on one of the backbone fins; if it nearly comes off with a little tug, the fish is done.

Makes 2 to 6 servings, depending on size of fish

Variation: A more complex version involves marinating the fish in olive oil, parsley, 2 finely chopped garlic cloves, and 1/4 cup lemon juice for 2 hours. More additions can be made, combining one or more of the following: crumbled bay leaves, red pepper flakes, fennel seeds, oregano, and rosemary.

Grilled Red Snapper

Grilled Sardine "Sausages"

"Sasizzeddi di Sarde Arrustuti"

This recipe from Palermo in Sicily is in great demand when I grill for friends. It is a preparation for a midsummer barbecue or whenever you find fresh sardines.

2 pounds fresh sardines (20 to 24), cleaned and gutted, with heads and tails removed

1/2 cup white wine vinegar

2 tablespoons olive oil

3/4 cup toasted bread crumbs

1/3 cup finely diced caciocavallo cheese

1 1/2 tablespoons currants, soaked in tepid water 15 minutes and drained

1 garlic clove, peeled and finely chopped

1 1/2 tablespoons chopped parsley

1 tablespoon pine nuts

Salt and freshly ground black pepper

2 large eggs

All-purpose flour for coating

3 Florida juice oranges

1 loaf crusty French baguette bread with crust on

1. Prepare a hot charcoal fire or preheat a gas grill for 15 minutes on high.

2. Pull out the backbones of the sardines by gripping the end of the backbone nearest to where the head was. Do this carefully so you do not rip the sardines in half. Wash each sardine with cold water, inside and out, and pat dry. Place the sardines in a 9 × 12-inch ceramic or glass baking pan and add the vinegar.

3. In a small frying pan, heat the olive oil over medium-high heat. Add 3 of the sardines and cook, stirring, until they disintegrate, 3 to 5 minutes. Add the bread crumbs, stirring with a wooden spoon until they are moistened. Add the cheese, drained currants, garlic, chopped parsley, and pine nuts. Season to taste with salt and pepper. Cook, stirring, for about 2 minutes. Remove from the heat.

4. Stuff each remaining sardine with a teaspoon of the bread crumb mixture. Squeeze closed, holding the sardines in your hands as if you were praying. Don't worry if they don't pinch shut. Set aside. You can also open the sardines and lay flat (they will be delta-shaped), spread some stuffing on them, and roll up from head to tail.

**Twelve 8- to 10-inch wooden
   skewers**

Olive oil for drizzling

Lemon wedges

Parsley sprigs for garnish

5. Beat the eggs in a shallow bowl. Spread some flour on a piece of wax paper. Carefully coat each sardine in egg, then dredge in the flour. Transfer to a baking tray. Shake the tray once, sharply, to shake off excess flour from the sardines without handling them too much.

6. Slice the oranges into cubes or 1×3-inch shapes, leaving the peel on. Slice the bread into cubes the same size and shape. Double skewer all the ingredients: hold 2 skewers parallel to each other about $^1/_2$ inch apart between your thumb and forefinger. Thread a sardine onto double skewers, then add a slice of bread and a slice of orange. Continue in that order, placing 2 sardines on each set of double skewers. Keep the split part of the sardine up so the stuffing doesn't fall out. (You need not worry about this if you have rolled the sardines.) When you lift the sardines from the tray to the skewers, use both hands and squeeze the sardines a bit. Once they are on the skewer, squeeze them with the bread and orange slices so all the pieces are tight against each other.

7. Drizzle olive oil over the skewers, place on the grill, and cook until some of the bread begins to blacken, about 5 minutes on each side. Serve with the lemon wedges and parsley sprigs. Don't discard the oranges and their peels. You eat everything!

Makes 4 to 6 servings

Grilled Sardines

"Sarde alla Griglia"

Fresh sardines, simply grilled as in this recipe, are a favorite of many southern Italians. Only very fresh sardines, which you should be able to find in an Italian ethnic neighborhood, work for this preparation. Fresh frozen sardines, thawed in the refrigerator over 2 days, will also work, although a little less satisfactorily. You could use smelts or whiting, but they are neither so flavorful nor so unique in taste as the sardines.

Olive oil

Salt

2 pounds fresh sardines (about 20 to 24), cleaned and gutted, with heads and tails on

Lemon wedges

1. Prepare a hot charcoal fire or preheat a gas grill for 15 minutes on high.

2. Lightly oil and salt the fish and place on the grill for 3 minutes on each side. Turn only once and leave the sardines undisturbed while they grill. Serve with lemon wedges and, if desired, olive oil.

Makes 4 to 6 servings

Variation 1: If fresh anchovies are available, remove their heads and gut them. Stir together some olive oil, lemon juice, finely chopped garlic, and salt. Coat the anchovies and grill for 2 to 3 minutes on each side.

Variation 2: With sardines or anchovies, leave the heads on after gutting and stuff with a mixture of finely chopped tomato, fennel leaves, olive oil, salt, and pepper.

Calabria-Style Grilled Mackerel with Anchovy Butter

"Sgrombri Grigliati alla Calabrese"

This delicious recipe from Calabria is quite rich and is perfect accompanied by a simple spaghetti.

Four 1-pound mackerel, cleaned and gutted, heads and tails removed, and cut into $3/4$-inch steaks

Olive oil for grilling

16 salted anchovy fillets (about 2 ounces), rinsed

$1/4$ cup ($1/2$ stick) unsalted butter, softened

3 tablespoons finely chopped fresh parsley

$1 1/4$ teaspoons freshly squeezed lemon juice

1. Prepare a hot charcoal fire or preheat a gas grill for 15 minutes on high.

2. Rub the mackerel steaks with the olive oil. (If you like, save the heads and tails for making fish stock.) Place the fish on the grill and cook, turning once, until the skin is blackened and crispy, about 8 minutes on each side.

3. Meanwhile, mash the anchovies, butter, parsley, and lemon juice in a bowl until very well blended.

4. Remove the mackerel steaks from the grill and transfer to a heated platter. Dot the top of each steak with anchovy butter and serve.

Makes 4 servings

Variation: In the anchovy butter, replace the parsley with mint and add $1/4$ teaspoon cayenne pepper.

Grilled Mackerel à la "Burnt Fingers"

"Sgrombri Grigliati a Scottadito"

*P*esce a scotàdeo *in Venetian, which means "burnt fingers fish," gives you the idea of how to eat this dish. Besides mackerel, you can use a mixture of sardines, red mullet, and other small fish.*

Four 1- to 1 ¹/₄-pound mackerel, cleaned and gutted, heads and tails on

¹/₄ cup olive oil

Salt and freshly ground black pepper

Juice of 1 lemon

1. Place the fish in a 9 × 12-inch ceramic or glass baking pan with the olive oil, salt and pepper to taste, and the lemon juice. Leave to marinate in the refrigerator, covered, for 2 hours, turning once or twice. Remove the fish from the refrigerator 15 minutes before grilling.

2. Prepare a hot charcoal fire or preheat a gas grill for 15 minutes on high.

3. Remove the fish from the marinade and reserve the marinade. Salt and pepper the fish again and place on the grill. Cook, turning once, until the skin is blackened and crispy, about 8 minutes on each side. Baste during grilling with the reserved marinade.

Makes 4 servings

Grilled Mackerel à la "Burnt Fingers"; grilled figs

Grilled Skewered Tuna

" 'Spitini' di Tonno"

Sicilians are fond of grilling skewered tuna and other foods. In this preparation the tuna pieces are double skewered with an intermingling of country bread, onions, and bay leaves.

Twelve 10-inch wooden skewers

1 to 2 onions, peeled, quartered, and separated

18 bay leaves, soaked in tepid water for 30 minutes if not fresh

About 2 pounds fresh tuna steak, cut into twenty-four 1-inch cubes

Twenty-four 1-inch cubes Italian country bread or French baguette

Salt and freshly ground black pepper

Olive oil for brushing

Bread crumbs for dredging

1. Prepare a hot charcoal fire or preheat a gas grill for 15 minutes on high.

2. Double skewer the ingredients: hold 2 skewers parallel to each other about ½ inch apart between your thumb and forefinger. Skewer the onion, bay leaf, tuna, and bread, in that order, until all the ingredients are used up. Use no more than 3 pieces of tuna per double skewer. Salt and pepper the skewers to taste. Brush each skewer on all sides liberally with olive oil. Spread the bread crumbs out on a large plate and dredge the skewers in the crumbs, coating all sides.

3. Drizzle some olive oil on the side of the skewer going face down on the grill. Place the skewers on the grill and cook without turning or moving for 5 minutes. Turn only once and grill another 5 minutes, basting all the time with olive oil. When the skewers are done, they will have blackened edges and an appetizing golden sheen. Remove the skewers before serving, or let your guests do it, and discard the bay leaves.

Makes 6 to 8 servings

Grilled Tuna with Red Salmoriglio Sauce

"Tonno Arrosto con Salmoriglio Rosso"

A simple grilled tuna topped with a squirt of lemon is typical of Sardinia and Sicily. But on the west coast of Sicily they use this sauce, called salmoriglio rosso, *although some call it* pesto Trapanese *to make people think of the famous* pesto Genovese.

¹/₄ cup olive oil, plus additional for dipping

2 pounds fresh tuna, cut into ³/₄-inch-thick steaks

Salt

Lemon wedges

2 ripe tomatoes, peeled, seeded, and drained well

2 to 3 garlic cloves, peeled

Handful of fresh parsley leaves

1 tablespoon white wine vinegar

1 teaspoon dried oregano

Freshly ground black pepper

1. Prepare a hot charcoal fire or preheat a gas grill for 15 minutes on high.

2. Pour some olive oil on a large plate and dip each slice of tuna in it. Place the tuna on the grill and cook, turning only once, until deep black grid marks appear, 5 to 6 minutes on each side. Transfer to a serving platter or individual plates, salt, and serve with lemon wedges.

3. Meanwhile, put the tomatoes, garlic cloves, parsley, vinegar, ¹/₄ cup olive oil, oregano, and salt and pepper to taste in a food processor and pulse until completely mixed. Spoon this pesto over the grilled tuna steaks.

Makes 4 to 6 servings

Grilled Tuna in Rosemary and Garlic, Palermo Style

"Tonno alla Palermitana"

A great summer grilling idea! Although Sicilians wouldn't traditionally serve the tuna medium-rare, I think it's better that way. Sicilians would typically make incisions in the tuna and stuff them with sage, rosemary, and garlic before grilling. You can do this too or follow the recipe below.

6 fresh tuna steaks, ³/₄ inch thick (about 2 pounds total)

1 cup dry white wine

4 small fresh sage leaves, finely chopped

1 sprig fresh rosemary, finely chopped

1 garlic clove, peeled and finely chopped

Juice of 2 lemons

¹/₄ cup finely chopped fresh parsley

¹/₄ cup olive oil

Salt and freshly ground black pepper

1. Place the tuna steaks in a 9×12-inch ceramic or glass baking pan and add the wine, sage, rosemary, and garlic. Leave to marinate in the refrigerator, covered, for 1 hour, turning frequently. Stir together the lemon juice and parsley and set aside. Remove the fish from the refrigerator 15 minutes before grilling.

2. Prepare a hot charcoal fire or preheat a gas grill for 15 minutes on high.

3. Drain the tuna, saving several tablespoons of marinade. Pat the tuna dry with paper towels. Dip the tuna slices in a plate filled with the olive oil, salt, and pepper and leave until needed.

4. Place the tuna slices on the grill and cook, basting constantly with the oil, leftover wine marinade, and lemon juice and parsley mix, until deep black grid marks appear, 3 to 4 minutes on each side.

Makes 4 to 6 servings

Grilled Tuna in Rosemary and Garlic, Palermo Style; sautéed broccoli rabe with red pepper

Grilled Tuna with a Parsley-Mint Coating

"Tonno alla Griglia"

This is a Sicilian-style grill preparation in which you will want to use the highest-quality tuna. The tuna steaks are dredged in garlic and herbed bread crumbs to form a coat that will become crisp and golden when grilled.

6 fresh tuna steaks, ³/₄ inch thick (about 2 pounds total)

¹/₄ cup olive oil

Salt and freshly ground black pepper

1 cup bread crumbs

1 garlic clove, peeled and finely chopped

1 tablespoon finely chopped fresh parsley

1 tablespoon finely chopped fresh mint

Lemon wedges

1. Prepare a hot charcoal fire or preheat a gas grill for 15 minutes on high.

2. Rub the tuna steaks on both sides with some of the olive oil, and salt and pepper to taste. Mix together the bread crumbs, garlic, parsley, and mint. Dredge the fish in this mixture.

3. Drizzle each tuna steak with some olive oil and place on the grill. Cook, turning only once, until deep black grid marks appear, about 5 minutes on each side. Serve with lemon wedges.

Makes 4 to 6 servings

Variation: Marinate the tuna in 1 cup dry white wine, ¹/₄ cup olive oil, salt, and pepper for 2 hours before dredging.

Grilled Tuna "Origanata"

"Tonno 'Riganatu'"

This Sicilian recipe is also excellent with halibut, bonito, or shrimp. Be sure not to overcook tuna, because it becomes unpleasantly dry.

1 pound fresh tuna steak, sliced
  $1/4$ inch thick

$1/4$ cup olive oil

1 garlic clove, peeled and finely
  chopped

Salt and freshly ground black
  pepper

3 tablespoons dried oregano

1. Place the tuna slices in a 9×12-inch ceramic or glass baking pan, add the olive oil, garlic, salt and pepper to taste, and oregano. Leave to marinate, covered, in the refrigerator for 2 hours. Remove the fish from the refrigerator 15 minutes before grilling.

2. Prepare a hot charcoal fire or preheat a gas grill for 15 minutes on high.

3. Remove the tuna from the marinade, reserving the marinade. Place the tuna slices on the grill and cook, basting with the marinade, until deep black grid marks appear, about 3 minutes on each side. Serve with the marinade. Grill longer if the fish is thicker.

Makes 2 to 3 servings

Marinated Grilled Tuna with a Bread-Crumb Coating

"Tonno Marinato alla Griglia"

A fresh tuna steak is marinated in wine, rosemary, and garlic, rolled in bread crumbs, which become a delicious golden, and then drizzled with anchovy-flavored olive oil. This recipe from Sicily is often called tonno alla siciliana *in the rest of Italy.*

6 fresh tuna steaks, ³/₄ inch thick (about 2 pounds total)

1 ¹/₂ cups dry white wine

Juice of 1 lemon

6 tablespoons olive oil

1 sprig fresh rosemary

1 garlic clove, peeled and finely chopped

Salt and freshly ground black pepper

1 cup bread crumbs

6 salted anchovy fillets, rinsed

1. Place the tuna steaks in a 9×12-inch ceramic or glass baking pan and add the wine, lemon juice, 2 tablespoons olive oil, rosemary, garlic, and salt and pepper to taste. Leave to marinate in the refrigerator, covered, for 2 hours. Remove the fish from the refrigerator 15 minutes before grilling.

2. Prepare a hot charcoal fire or preheat a gas grill for 15 minutes on high.

3. Drain the tuna and dredge in the bread crumbs. Drizzle both sides of the tuna steaks with a little olive oil. Place the tuna on the grill and cook, turning only once and basting with the marinade if desired until deep black grid marks appear, 4 to 5 minutes on each side.

4. Meanwhile, melt the anchovy fillets in the remaining olive oil in a small pan over medium-high heat, stirring with a wooden spoon. As soon as they have melted, spoon the anchovy sauce over the grilled tuna steaks and serve.

Makes 4 to 6 servings

Variation: For an even simpler preparation, omit the bread crumbs and serve the fish with lemon wedges.

Grilled Tuna with a Fennel-Seed Coating

"Tonno ai Ferri"

This specialty from Trieste is sprinkled with crushed fennel seeds before grilling. If your tuna is very fresh, as it should be, with blood still visible, soak in cold water for 20 minutes before preparing. In Calabria and Basilicata they grill trout in the same manner.

4 fresh tuna steaks, 1 inch thick (about 2 pounds total)

1 tablespoon fennel seeds, crushed in a mortar

Salt and freshly ground white pepper

3 tablespoons olive oil

1. Prepare a hot charcoal fire or preheat a gas grill for 15 minutes on high.

2. Sprinkle the tuna with the fennel seeds and salt and pepper to taste. Moisten with olive oil on both sides. Place the tuna steaks on the grill and cook, sprinkled with a bit more fennel seeds if desired, until deep black grid marks appear, 6 to 7 minutes on each side.

Makes 4 to 6 servings

Variation: Marinate the tuna for 1 hour with the fennel seeds, 2 tablespoons finely chopped fresh parsley, the olive oil, and 2 tablespoons lemon juice before grilling.

Grilled Tuna with Wine and Thyme Marinade

"Tonno alla 'Graèla'"

This is an old Venetian recipe for grilling the dark meat of tuna. A graèla is a cast-iron grid used for grilling. Try the anchovy sauce—it's fantastic with grilled tuna—and accompany it with Grilled Stale Bread (page 170).

6 slices fresh tuna steaks, about $^3/_8$ inch thick (about 2 pounds total)

$^3/_4$ cup olive oil, plus additional for basting

2 cups white wine

1 onion, peeled and very thinly sliced

3 tablespoons finely chopped fresh parsley

1 teaspoon dried thyme

1 bay leaf, crumbled

Salt and freshly ground black pepper

1. Place the tuna steaks in a 9×12-inch ceramic or glass baking pan and add the olive oil, white wine, onion, parsley, thyme, bay leaf, and salt and pepper to taste. Leave to marinate in the refrigerator, covered, for 2 hours, turning once. Remove the fish from the refrigerator 15 minutes before grilling.

2. Prepare a hot charcoal fire or preheat a gas grill for 15 minutes on high.

3. Remove the tuna from the marinade and place on the grill. Cook, basting with olive oil and turning only once, until deep black grid marks appear, about $3^1/_2$ minutes on each side. Serve with Anchovy Sauce (below) if desired.

Makes 4 to 6 servings

Anchovy Sauce

Pound 4 rinsed salted anchovy fillets with 2 cloves of garlic and 2 tablespoons finely chopped fresh parsley to the consistency of a pesto, and then slowly beat or pound in 3 tablespoons olive oil and $^1/_2$ teaspoon freshly squeezed lemon juice. Spread over the grilled tuna steaks immediately and serve.

Tuscan-Style Grilled Marinated Red Mullet

"Triglie in Gratella alla Marinara"

In Tuscany, red mullet is prepared very simply in an aromatic marinade, but then it is breaded before grilling. The golden and crisp bread crumb coating holds in the flavorful juices. If you can't find red mullet, use another small fish or even red snapper.

8 red mullet (about 3 pounds total), scaled, cleaned and gutted, and patted dry with paper towels

$1/4$ cup olive oil

2 garlic cloves, peeled and finely chopped

2 sprigs fresh rosemary, leaves chopped

1 cup bread crumbs

Salt and freshly ground black pepper

Lemon wedges

1. Place the red mullet in a 9×12-inch ceramic or glass baking pan, add the olive oil, garlic, and rosemary, and leave to marinate in the refrigerator, covered, for 2 hours, turning once or twice. Remove the mullet from the refrigerator 15 minutes before grilling.

2. Prepare a hot charcoal fire or preheat a gas grill for 15 minutes on high.

3. Drain the mullet. Spread the bread crumbs on a large plate and dredge the fish in them. Place the mullet on the grill and cook, turning once, until the skin is blackened a bit and crispy or peeling, about 7 to 8 minutes on each side. Salt and pepper to taste and serve with lemon wedges.

Makes 4 servings

Spicy Abruzzi-Style Grilled Red Mullet

"Triglie sulla Graticola"

In the Abruzzo, fish are grilled on reed skewers pushed through the mouth and out the tail and set over the burning embers of a hardwood fire. You can grill them the same way with long metal skewers or simply use a hinged fish griller. If red mullet is not available, use two of any fresh whole 2 ½-pound fish. Make the fish as hot as you wish with the cayenne pepper.

12 red mullet (about 5 pounds), scaled, cleaned and gutted, and patted dry with paper towels

¹⁄₃ cup olive oil

3 tablespoons finely chopped fresh parsley

2 bay leaves, crumbled

1 teaspoon fresh thyme leaves

Cayenne pepper

Freshly ground black pepper

1. Place the fish in a 9 × 12-inch ceramic or glass baking pan and add the olive oil, parsley, bay leaves, thyme, cayenne, and black pepper to taste. Leave to marinate in the refrigerator for 2 hours, turning once or twice. If using larger fish, score in 2 or 3 places. Remove the fish from the refrigerator 15 minutes before grilling.

2. Prepare a hot charcoal fire or preheat a gas grill for 15 minutes on high.

3. Remove the fish from the marinade, reserving the marinade. Place the fish on the grill and cook until the skin is blackened a bit and crispy or peeling, 7 to 8 minutes on each side. Baste with the marinade during grilling.

Makes 6 servings

Variation: Make a marinade by mixing ¹⁄₄ cup finely chopped fresh parsley, 1 tablespoon dried oregano, 2 finely chopped garlic cloves, and 2 crumbled bay leaves together. Stir in ¹⁄₄ cup olive oil, ¹⁄₂ cup white wine, and salt and pepper to taste.

Spicy Abruzzi-Style Grilled Red Mullet; Spaghetti with Red Chili Pepper (page 176)

Grilled Red Mullet with Shrimp Sauce

"Triglie ai Ferri in Salsa di Gamberetti"

The flavorful relish, or gremolada, *a special mixture put on food after it has been cooked, is perfect for mild-tasting fish. Here I use the traditional red mullet, which can be found in good ethnic, especially Italian or Greek, fish stores in urban areas. In its place you can use red snapper, redfish, or grouper.*

2 cooked jumbo shrimp (see Note)

¹/₄ cup unsalted butter

2 tablespoons olive oil

1 teaspoon finely chopped fresh parsley

1 teaspoon finely chopped capers

2 teaspoons very finely chopped onion

1 teaspoon Dijon mustard

1 teaspoon freshly squeezed lemon juice

12 red mullet (about 5 pounds), scaled, cleaned, and gutted, heads and tails left on; or 2 pounds red snapper, redfish, or grouper fillets

Salt

1. Prepare a hot charcoal fire or preheat a gas grill for 15 minutes on high.

2. Prepare a shrimp butter with the shrimp and 2 tablespoons of the butter by processing in short bursts or pounding in a mortar until thoroughly blended. Set aside, covered, in the refrigerator. Melt the remaining butter and keep warm.

3. Prepare the *gremolada* by mixing together the olive oil, parsley, capers, onion, mustard, shrimp butter, and lemon juice. Mix well. Alternatively, you can prepare it in a blender or food processor.

4. Brush the mullet or fish fillets with the melted butter and salt lightly. Place the fish on the grill, 5 to 6 inches from the fire. Grill, turning only once, until the skin is blackened a bit and crispy or peeling, 7 to 8 minutes on each side. Transfer to a serving platter and spread about 1 teaspoon of *gremolada* on each fish. If using fish fillets you need to grill them on an oiled grill topper (if your grilling grates are too wide) until golden and almost flaking, about 7 to 10 minutes a side for ³/₄-inch-thick fillets.

Makes 4 to 6 servings

Note: Cook the shrimp in rapidly boiling salted water for 2 minutes; drain, cool, shell, and use as required in step 2.

Whole Fish on the Grill

Whole fish can be cooked on the grill, using a hinged fish grill or grill topper (a perforated metal sheet that lies on the grill) if the spaces between the grids of your grilling grate are too wide. The grilling grate, grill topper, or hinged fish grill (also called a fish basket) should be oiled and very hot. The fish should be oiled too so that it will not stick.

One rule of thumb to remember for grilling whole fish to perfect doneness is to count 10 minutes per inch of thickness measured at the thickest part of the fish.

Some people score the fish with a sharp knife. It is not necessary but it is attractive.

Grilled Swordfish

"Pesce Spada alla Griglia"

Here it is! The Sicilian grilled swordfish that all those returned travelers rave about. It is a simple favorite, and although there are many variations on the marinade, the result still depends on the quality of the swordfish. You don't have to go to Sicily to find that fabled swordfish—the best I ever had came from Wellfleet on Cape Cod one late August day.

2 pounds swordfish steaks, sliced either 1 inch thick or ³/₈ inch thick

Marinade 1:

¹/₄ cup olive oil

Juice of 1 lemon

1 tablespoon finely chopped fresh mint

1 teaspoon dried oregano

Salt and freshly ground black pepper

Marinade 2:

¹/₄ cup olive oil

Juice of 1 lemon

2 garlic cloves, peeled and finely chopped

2 tablespoons finely chopped fresh parsley

Salt and freshly ground black pepper

1. Place the swordfish in a 9 × 12-inch ceramic or glass baking pan. Combine the ingredients for the marinade of your choice and pour over the swordfish. Leave to marinate in the refrigerator, covered, for 4 hours, turning once or twice. Remove the fish 15 minutes before grilling.

2. Prepare a hot charcoal fire or preheat a gas grill for 15 minutes on high.

3. Remove the swordfish from the marinade, reserving the marinade. Place the swordfish on the grill and cook, basting with the marinade, until deep black grid marks appear. Grill the ³/₈-inch steaks 4 minutes on each side, and the thicker steaks 6 minutes on each side.

Makes 4 to 6 servings

Variation 1: My friend Chef Carlo Middione, owner of the Vivande Ristorante in San Francisco, likes to roll thin swordfish slices up into cigar shapes and coat each slice with a mixture of ³/₄ cup fresh bread

Grilled Swordfish; Spaghetti with Parsley and Anchovy (page 177)

crumbs, 4 very finely chopped garlic cloves, 1 teaspoon dried oregano, and salt to taste. He oils each slice before rolling, secures it with a toothpick, and grills the rolls about 6 inches over a wood fire for 8 minutes.

Variation 2: Prepare the Sauce for Grilled Fish (page 202), Mixed Mayonnaise for Grilled Fish or Chicken (page 201), and Devil's Hot Sauce (page 197). Place a small dollop of each on a large individual dinner plate and serve with a 4-inch square of grilled swordfish and one of grilled shark.

Pesce alla Griglia, Fish on the Grill

Many Italians consider grilling the finest way to prepare fish. In the simplest method the whole fish is laid on an oiled grilling grate, scales and all, brushed with a little olive oil, and grilled. The scales form a seal, holding in all the juices for a succulent grilled fish. After cooking, the scales peel off easily, and the fish is salted and peppered and served. This technique is not used for fatty fish such as salmon, mackerel, bluefish, sardines, and herring.

Traditionally, Italians grill their fish on an iron grate set over a shallow earthenware brazier filled with white-hot wood embers. The grilling grate is brushed with oil to prevent sticking. Sometimes a hinged double grill is used so that the fish or other fragile or small foods can be turned easily.

On the Adriatic, fish is grilled in a style called *alla moda dell'Adriatico*. Whiting, red mullet, gray mullet, John Dory, turbot, halibut, sole roll-ups, monkfish, cuttlefish, squid, or shrimp are marinated for a couple of hours in olive oil, garlic, parsley, salt, pepper, a few tablespoons of bread crumbs, and sometimes lemon juice and rosemary. The fish are scored and sometimes skewered before grilling. The shrimp are grilled in their shells. Finally, the grilled fish and shellfish are sprinkled with vinegar before they are served.

In Sardinia *naselli*, or hake, are cut up and skewered with bay leaves before grilling. Grilled octopus is not as popular in Italy as in Greece—but the

(continues)

(continued)

Sardinians grill it. If you do decide to grill an octopus, first boil a 2- to 3-pound octopus at a simmer for 1½ hours. Drain and peel off the skin. Marinate for 2 hours in olive oil, lemon juice, salt, and pepper, then grill for 10 minutes.

In Italy certain species of fish are favored for grilling whole, such as *aguglia* (garfish, an interesting pointy-nosed fish with green bones), *branzino* or *spigola* (sea bass), *rombo* (turbot), *pagro* (a kind of bream that can be replaced with porgies, also called scup, or butterfish), *orata* (gilt-head bream), *mormora* (striped bream, a rare fish with a delicate taste), and *muggine* or *cefalo* (gray mullet, which in Sardinia is also cut into steaks and skewered with bay leaves before grilling). *Dragone,* a Tuscan dialect word for *trancina* (weever), is a strange-looking fish with upward-gazing eyes. Although it is mostly used for broths and stews, the Tuscans also grill it. Of the freshwater fish, trout and perch are usually grilled.

Red mullet, or *triglia,* is a very popular fish that is grilled unadorned, except for a brushing of olive oil, over a hot fire and gutted only after cooking. It can also be served with anchovy butter on a piece of bruschetta or simply with bay leaves. In the United States, where red mullet is harder to find, red snapper can be substituted.

A favorite grilled fish, although expensive, is *dentice,* dentex (a kind of bream), a beautiful fish for the grill. All these fish are delicious and can occasionally be found in North American fish markets, especially those run by ethnic fishmongers such as Greeks and Italians. If you should find any of the fish mentioned, marinate them in a mixture of olive oil, garlic, parsley, and rosemary for 2 hours before grilling. If you can't find any of these fish, choose the freshest available local fish.

Some fish to consider for grilling whole are red snapper, grouper, sea bass, bluefish, redfish, cod, hake, or whatever a good fishmonger recommends. Bigger fish, such as *cernia* (grouper), can be scored first on both sides. Fish steaks, such as swordfish or tuna, can be coated with bread crumbs and grilled with a drizzle of olive oil.

Grilled Swordfish with Marinade and Sardine-Cayenne Pesto

"Grigliata di Pesce Spada"

I can't emphasize enough the importance of the fish in this recipe. The sauce is not meant to hide the taste of the fish but to enhance it, so your swordfish must be superlative, which means very fresh, at the height of the season between July and September.

1 cup olive oil

1 cup dry white wine

1 bay leaf, crumbled

1 medium-size onion, peeled and thinly sliced

Salt

8 black peppercorns

6 to 8 swordfish steaks, about 1 inch thick (about 3 pounds total)

2 garlic cloves, peeled and finely chopped

3 canned sardines, mashed

1 tablespoon dried oregano

$1/2$ teaspoon cayenne pepper

Juice of 1 lemon

6 to 8 lemon slices for garnish

Chopped parsley for garnish (optional)

1. In a large ceramic or glass dish, combine $3/4$ cup of the olive oil, the wine, bay leaf, onion, 1 teaspoon salt, and the peppercorns. Add the swordfish steaks and marinate in the refrigerator, covered, for 2 hours. Remove the fish from the refrigerator 15 minutes before grilling.

2. Heat 2 tablespoons of the olive oil in a small frying pan over low heat. Add the garlic and cook, stirring, until it is about to sizzle but before it begins to turn light brown, about 3 minutes. Add the sardines, oregano, cayenne, and $1/2$ teaspoon salt. With the back of a wooden spoon, mix and mash into a paste. Remove the pan from the heat and stir in the remaining 2 tablespoons olive oil and the lemon juice. Add more salt to taste. Mix well and keep warm.

3. Prepare a hot charcoal fire or preheat a gas grill for 15 minutes on high.

4. Remove the swordfish from the marinade, reserving the marinade. Place the swordfish on the grill and cook for 5 minutes on one side. Brush with marinade and turn to the other side. Brush again with

marinade and grill until blackened grid marks appear, another 5 minutes.

5. Remove the swordfish and serve with the sardine mixture. Garnish each steak with a slice of lemon and chopped parsley, if desired.

Makes 6 to 8 servings

Grilled Stuffed Swordfish Rolls

"Involtini di Pesce Spada"

Swordfish is immensely popular in Sicily, where this preparation for grilled swordfish brings you just a little closer to heaven.

The swordfish needs to be sliced thinly, which is easily done if it is partially frozen (but don't freeze completely and thaw). Choose a filling and experience grilled Sicilian involtini *of swordfish.*

This filling is typical of a style of Sicilian cooking called cucina arabo-sicula, *the cooking derived from the influence of the medieval Arab era in Sicily. The first variation is typical of the* monzù, *the French-influenced master chefs who served the nineteenth-century Sicilian aristocracy, while the second variation is a popular one in Calabria, the toe of the Italian "boot."*

2 ¹/₂ pounds swordfish steaks, cut into ten to twelve ¹/₄-inch-thick slices

Olive oil for dipping and drizzling

1. Flatten the swordfish slices further between 2 pieces of wax paper, pounding with the side of a mallet or heavy cleaver very gently so you don't break the flesh. Each slice should be about 5 ¹/₂ × 3 ¹/₂ inches.

Filling:

2 tablespoons olive oil

1 medium-size onion, peeled and finely chopped

1 ³/₄ cups bread crumbs

2 salted anchovy fillets, rinsed and chopped

1 large garlic clove, peeled and finely chopped

2 tablespoons pine nuts

1 tablespoon golden raisins or currants

2 tablespoons freshly grated pecorino cheese

1 tablespoon freshly squeezed lemon juice

1 tablespoon freshly squeezed orange juice

1 large egg, beaten

Salt and freshly ground black pepper

Coating:

1 large egg, beaten

2 tablespoons olive oil

1 cup bread crumbs

2 tablespoons freshly grated caciocavallo or pecorino cheese

¹/₂ teaspoon dried oregano

2. Prepare the filling: heat the olive oil in a medium-size frying pan over medium heat. Add the onion and cook, stirring, until translucent, about 7 minutes. Combine the cooked onion with the bread crumbs, anchovies, garlic, pine nuts, raisins or currants, pecorino, lemon juice, orange juice, and egg. Mix well and salt and pepper to taste. Divide the filling among the swordfish slices and roll up, folding in the edges and squeezing the rolled *involtini* in your hands. Secure any opening with toothpicks. Dip the *involtini* in olive oil.

3. Prepare the coating: stir the beaten egg and the 2 tablespoons olive oil together and set aside. Combine the bread crumbs, caciocavallo or pecorino, oregano, parsley, garlic, and salt and pepper to taste. Dredge the swordfish rolls in the egg mixture and then roll in the bread crumb mixture to coat lightly.

4. Prepare a hot charcoal fire or preheat a gas grill for 15 minutes on high.

5. Double skewer all the ingredients: hold 2 skewers parallel to each other about ¹/₂ inch apart between your thumb and forefinger. Slide the *involtini* interspersed with bay leaves and onion sections onto each set of skewers, putting 2 *involtini* on each set, and drizzle with olive oil. Place the skewers on the grill and cook for about 6 minutes on each side. Serve with lemon wedges.

Makes 6 servings

1 tablespoon finely chopped
  fresh parsley

1 garlic clove, very finely
  chopped

Salt and freshly ground black
  pepper

Garnishes for grilling:

30 bay leaves, soaked in tepid
  water for 30 minutes

3 large onions, quartered and
  separated

Twelve 10-inch wooden skewers

Lemon wedges

Variation 1: Replace step 2 with the following: Heat ¼ cup olive oil in a medium-size frying pan over medium-high heat. Add 1 pound finely chopped boneless, skinless, swordfish steak and 1 cup finely chopped onion and cook, stirring, for 5 minutes. Drizzle in 6 tablespoons brandy and salt to taste. When the brandy has evaporated, remove the filling to a mixing bowl and stir in 6 tablespoons bread crumbs. Divide the filling among the swordfish slices. Lay one of 12 slices of mozzarella (about 1 pound) on each swordfish slice. Divide 1 tablespoon finely chopped fresh basil and 1 teaspoon fresh or dried thyme among the slices and pepper them all to taste. Roll up the slices, folding in the edges and squeezing the rolled *involtini* in your hands. Secure any openings with toothpicks. Dip the *involtini* in olive oil. Omit step 3 and the bay leaf and onion garnishes.

Variation 2: Replace step 2 with the following: Mix 1¾ cups bread crumbs; 2 tablespoons dried oregano; 4 garlic cloves, peeled and finely chopped; ¼ cup capers; ¼ cup freshly grated pecorino cheese; 2 tablespoons finely chopped fresh parsley; and 2 tablespoons freshly squeezed lemon juice. Salt the swordfish slices and dip them in olive oil. Divide the stuffing among the swordfish slices. Roll up the slices, folding in the edges and squeezing the rolled *involtini* in your hands. Secure any openings with toothpicks. Omit step 3 and the bay leaf and onion garnishes.

Mixed Fish Grill with Three Sauces

"Misto Griglia di Pesce con Tre Salse"

The idea here is very simple and very satisfying. Three different kinds of fish are lightly drizzled with olive oil and grilled. Three dollops of the sauces are placed on a large individual serving plate with the grilled fish for a delightful "tasting menu."

Here's a chance to try some fish you may not normally eat. My favorite choices are swordfish, mako shark, and monkfish or dogfish, which I have also found marketed as Cape shark. You can try any firm-fleshed fish, such as salmon, tuna, or grouper. Each 1-pound fish steak is grilled in one piece and divided to serve.

1 pound swordfish steak

1 pound mako shark steak

1 pound dogfish steak

Olive oil for drizzling

Salt and freshly ground black pepper

1 recipe Sauce for Grilled Fish (page 202)

1 recipe Mixed Mayonnaise Sauce for Grilled Fish or Chicken (page 201)

1 recipe Devil's Hot Sauce (page 197)

1. Prepare a hot charcoal fire or preheat a gas grill for 15 minutes on high.

2. Drizzle both sides of the fish with olive oil and salt and pepper to taste. Place the fish on the grill and cook until black grid marks appear, about 5 minutes on each side, turning only once. Serve alone or with the sauces.

Makes 6 servings

Note: Reserve and refrigerate any remaining sauce or mayonnaise.

Grilled Salmon Steaks with Oregano Pesto

"Salmone alla Griglia con Pesto Origanato"

Salmon is not a common fish among Italians because of expense and lack of availability. But luckily for us, salmon is readily found here. It's a rich fish that grills perfectly, and in this recipe it is coated with an oregano pesto.

1 1/2 cups loosely packed fresh oregano leaves, rinsed and dried completely

3 garlic cloves, peeled

1 teaspoon very finely chopped pork or bacon fat (optional)

1 tablespoon pine nuts

1/4 cup olive oil

Salt and freshly ground black pepper

4 salmon steaks (about 2 pounds)

Bread crumbs for dredging

1. In a mortar, pound the oregano leaves, garlic, pork fat (if using), and pine nuts until mushy. Slowly pour in the olive oil in a thin stream while continuing to pound until you have a pesto. Salt and pepper to taste.

2. Place the salmon steaks in a 9 × 12-inch ceramic or glass baking pan, coat with the pesto on both sides, then dredge in the bread crumbs. Leave to rest in the refrigerator, covered, for 30 minutes. Remove the fish from the refrigerator 15 minutes before grilling.

3. Prepare a hot charcoal fire or preheat a gas grill for 15 minutes on high.

4. Place the salmon steaks on the grill and cook, turning only once, until the fatty edges are crispy and the salmon looks like it will flake, about 6 to 7 minutes on each side.

Makes 4 to 6 servings

Milk-Marinated Grilled Smoked Herring

"Aringa alla Griglia"

This is an old recipe from the fish cookery of the Veneto region. Because the fish could be preserved, it was popular as part of the cuisine of the poor, cucina povera, *and was served with Grilled Polenta (page 168).*

1 ¹/₂ pounds smoked herring fillet, skin removed if desired

2 cups milk

¹/₄ cup olive oil

2 tablespoons finely chopped fresh parsley

Salt and freshly ground black pepper

1. Split the smoked herring, if whole, and then cut in half. Place the herring in a 9 × 12-inch ceramic or glass baking pan and add the milk. Leave to marinate in the refrigerator, covered, for 4 hours, turning once. Remove the fish from the refrigerator 30 minutes before grilling.

2. Place the herring on the grill and cook, turning once, until golden, about 5 minutes on each side. Slice into serving portions and arrange on a serving platter, pour the olive oil over, and sprinkle with the parsley and salt and pepper to taste.

Makes 4 to 6 servings as an appetizer

Grilled Skewered Scallops and Shrimp

"Spiedini di Cape Sante e Gamberetti"

Grill these skewers of shrimp and scallops until the shrimp are orange and the scallops are light golden brown. Make sure the pieces toward the center of the skewer are grilled through by spacing the scallops and shrimp on the skewer so that they don't touch each other.

1 pound medium-size shrimp, shelled

1 pound sea scallops

Juice of 1 orange

$1/2$ cup dry white wine

$1/4$ cup olive oil

$1/4$ cup finely chopped fresh oregano or 1 tablespoon dried

Freshly ground black pepper

Six 10-inch wooden skewers

1. Place the shrimp and scallops in a 9×12-inch ceramic or glass baking pan and add the orange juice, white wine, olive oil, oregano, and pepper to taste. Leave to marinate in the refrigerator, covered, for 2 hours. Remove from the refrigerator 15 minutes before grilling.

2. Prepare a hot charcoal fire or preheat a gas grill for 15 minutes on high.

3. Remove the shrimp and scallops from the marinade, reserving the marinade. Skewer the shrimp and scallops so they don't touch. Place on the grill and cook, turning occasionally, until the shrimp are orange and the scallops a light golden brown, about 20 minutes. Baste with the marinade during grilling.

Makes 4 servings

Grilled Shrimp

"Scampi alla Griglia"

Grilling shrimp is a very simple matter that can easily go wrong. The difference between succulent shrimp grilled to golden orange perfection and dry, withered buttons of nothing is a matter of a minute or so. When grilling shrimp, it is best to stay by the fire and keep your eyes on them, turning often and poking them with your finger to test for doneness. Use any size shrimp if the ones I call for are not available.

16 super-colossal shrimp (about 10 to a pound), unpeeled

Olive oil for brushing or drizzling

Salt

Five 8-inch wooden skewers

A brush made of rosemary sprigs (optional)

Lemon wedges

1. Prepare a hot charcoal fire or preheat a gas grill for 15 minutes on high.

2. Skewer the shrimp in their shells through the top part of the body and the tail. Brush the shrimp with olive oil and salt to taste. Place on the grill and cook for 7 minutes, turning occasionally. Remove from the grill and crush very lightly with a rolling pin or heavy object to make the shells easier to remove.

3. Continue grilling the shrimp for another 7 minutes, brushing or drizzling with olive oil when necessary, and using the rosemary brush if desired. Serve the shrimp in their shells with lemon wedges.

Makes 4 servings

Grilled Shrimp; Tagliatelle with Garlic, Olive Oil, and Raw Tomatoes (page 180)

Variation 1: For convenience, remove the shells before serving, if desired.

Variation 2: Before grilling, shell the shrimp and marinate for 2 hours in ¼ cup olive oil, 2 finely chopped garlic cloves, 2 tablespoons finely chopped fresh parsley, 1 teaspoon finely chopped fresh sage, and salt and pepper to taste.

Variation 3: Before grilling, shell the shrimp and marinate for 2 hours in ¼ cup dry white wine, 3 tablespoons olive oil, 2 tablespoons finely chopped fresh parsley, and salt and pepper to taste. Thread, interspersed with bay leaves, onto a skewer.

Shrimp or Lobster?

If you have ever had grilled scampi in Italy and wonder why you can't seem to re-create the taste back home with shrimp, it's because most of us have access only to frozen shrimp. When thawing shrimp, do it slowly in the refrigerator over 2 days rather than buying the defrosted shrimp sold in the supermarkets (they usually defrost too fast). Also, scampi are a kind of lobster so saying "shrimp scampi" is nonsensical.

Grilled Skewered Shrimp and Squid

"Spiedini di Mare alla Griglia"

Once these skewered pieces of shrimp and squid are grilled, they take on a beautiful orange color that I find very appetizing. If any shrimp or squid seem to have a little light purple color to them, especially the pieces in the center of the skewer, continue grilling a few minutes more.

1 pound medium-size shrimp, shelled

1 pound squid, cleaned, bodies split open lengthwise and quartered

$1/4$ cup olive oil

1 garlic clove, peeled and mashed

1 bay leaf, crumbled

Juice of 1 lemon

3 tablespoons finely chopped fresh parsley

Salt and freshly ground black pepper

Ten 8-inch wooden skewers

1. Place the shrimp and squid in a 9×12-inch ceramic or glass baking pan and add the olive oil, garlic, bay leaf, lemon juice, parsley, and salt and pepper to taste. Leave to marinate in the refrigerator, covered, for 2 hours. Remove from the refrigerator 15 minutes before grilling.

2. Prepare a hot charcoal fire or preheat a gas grill for 15 minutes on high.

3. Remove the shrimp and squid from the marinade, reserving the marinade. Skewer the shrimp and squid. Place on the grill and cook, basting with the marinade occasionally, until bright orange, 7 to 8 minutes on each side. Remove to a warm platter and serve.

Makes 4 servings

Variation: After the skewers are prepared, roll them in $1/2$ cup bread crumbs and drizzle with olive oil before grilling.

Grilled Stuffed Squid

"Calamari Ripieni"

The simplest way to grill squid is to clean them and marinate with olive oil, parsley, and salt and pepper for 1 hour, then grill for 20 to 30 minutes. For this stuffed version some people also add eggs or raisins or leave out the cheese. The Italians also eat cuttlefish, which they catch while still small. The cuttlefish available to us are much bigger and better suited to being cut up and grilled rather than stuffed.

8 large squid (1 to 1¹/₄ pounds), cleaned

6 tablespoons olive oil

1 cup bread crumbs

1 garlic clove, peeled and finely chopped

2 tablespoons finely chopped fresh parsley

Salt and freshly ground black pepper

3 ounces fresh mozzarella cheese, finely chopped

1 teaspoon dried oregano

1. Cut the tentacles off the squid below the eyes and chop the tentacles finely. Heat 3 tablespoons of the olive oil in a frying pan over medium heat, add the bread crumbs and chopped tentacles, and cook, stirring, until the bread crumbs begin to turn golden brown, about 7 minutes. Transfer to a mixing bowl and toss with the garlic, parsley, and salt and pepper to taste, mixing well. Toss again with the mozzarella.

2. Mix the remaining 3 tablespoons olive oil with the oregano and a pinch of salt and pepper.

3. Prepare a medium-hot charcoal fire or preheat a gas grill for 15 minutes on medium-high.

4. Dry the squid well. Stuff loosely with the filling and close the opening with a toothpick. Brush with the seasoned olive oil, place on the grill, and cook for 15 to 17 minutes on each side, basting with the seasoned olive oil occasionally. Or turn the stuffed squid frequently, cooking for a total of 35 minutes.

Makes 4 servings

Variation 1: After stuffing, leave the squid to marinate, covered, in the refrigerator for 2 hours in ¼ cup olive oil, 1 tablespoon vinegar, salt, and pepper.

Variation 2: In Sardinia cooks stuff the squid with 1 cup bread crumbs; 4 squid tentacles, boiled for 3 minutes and finely chopped; ¼ cup finely chopped parsley; 2 finely chopped garlic cloves; 6 finely chopped anchovy fillets; and salt and pepper to taste.

Grilled Oysters

"Ostriche Arrosto"

It may seem unusual to grill oysters, but this method is ideal for the bivalves—the bottom shell acts as a grill topper or holder. Clams are also excellent grilled. Grill them unopened in the shell, until they "yawn," 20 to 40 minutes. As the clams begin to open, their liquid will drip, causing the smoke to swirl around them until they are fully opened.

24 oysters in the shell

1 tablespoon baking soda

1 ½ cups bread crumbs

6 tablespoons finely chopped fresh parsley

2 garlic cloves, peeled and very finely chopped

Freshly ground black pepper

Juice of 1 lemon

Olive oil for drizzling

Salt

1. Soak the oysters in cold water with the baking soda for 2 hours. Remove the flat, top shell.

2. Prepare a hot charcoal fire or preheat a gas grill for 15 minutes on high.

3. Mix the bread crumbs, parsley, garlic, and black pepper, to taste, together and put a teaspoon or more on top of each oyster. Sprinkle a few drops of lemon juice on each oyster and drizzle with olive oil and salt and pepper to taste.

4. Place the oysters in the half shell on the grill and cook until the bread crumbs are golden and flecked with black, about 12 minutes.

Makes 4 to 6 servings

Lobster on the Grill

"Aragosta sulla Graticola"

This is a beautiful and delectable way to serve lobster. Remember that grilling can dry out a lobster quite quickly, so it is important to keep it well oiled or buttered.

Four 1 1/2-pound live lobsters (see Box, page 152)

1/4 cup (1/2 stick) unsalted butter (optional)

Olive oil

Salt and freshly ground black pepper

Bread crumbs

1 lemon

2 tablespoons finely chopped fresh parsley

1. Prepar a medium-hot charcoal fire or preheat a gas grill for 15 minutes on medium-high.

2. Split each lobster lengthwise with a heavy cleaver or large chef's knife, holding the crustacean firmly because it will move a lot. Crack the claws. Remove the greenish-gray tomalley and reserve for another use or whip into the butter and serve with the grilled lobster. Drizzle olive oil over both halves of each lobster. Salt and pepper to taste.

3. Place the lobsters shell side down on the grill and cook, basting with olive oil, for 15 minutes. Remove the lobster halves from the grill, drizzle the lobster meat with olive oil, and sprinkle bread crumbs to coat the meat. Drizzle the bread crumbs with more olive oil, pressing them down into the meat. Grill the lobsters bread-crumb side down until golden brown and crusty, about 15 more minutes. Turn over twice to baste with olive oil while you are grilling during the second 15 minutes.

4. Serve with a squirt of lemon juice, a sprinkle of parsley, and the tomalley butter, if using.

Makes 4 servings

Lobster on the Grill; herbed orzo

To Split a Lobster

Unless you're the kind of person who can drive a nail with one hammer blow, the best way to split a live lobster down the middle is to turn the lobster on its back, holding it around the upper body near the claws with an oven mitt or kitchen towel. Place the blade of a heavy cleaver lengthwise in the middle of the body. Let go of the body briefly and give the dull-edged top of the cleaver a few hard whacks with the palm of your hand to drive it through the body and shell, from head to tail. The lobster will not cooperate in this procedure, so remember to hold the body firmly and work quickly.

Grilled Seafood Salad

"Insalata di Mare"

This is quite an appetizing preparation. After grilling, the shrimp are a startling orange, the squid is golden, the octopus is lavender, the clams white, and the mussels yellow. It's all very beautiful and tastes even better. Both squid and octopus are usually sold already cleaned.

1 fresh octopus (about 2 pounds), cleaned

2 tablespoons white wine vinegar

1 cup olive oil

2 garlic cloves, peeled and finely chopped

$1/4$ cup finely chopped fresh parsley

24 mussels, scrubbed and bearded just before cooking

24 littleneck clams, scrubbed

24 small squid (about 2 pounds), cleaned

Salt and freshly ground black pepper

Four 10-inch wooden skewers

24 medium-size shrimp in the shell

1 to 3 tablespoons freshly squeezed lemon juice

1. Put the octopus in a medium-size pot and cover with cold water and the vinegar. Bring to a boil over high heat, reduce the heat to medium, and simmer, covered, until the octopus is firm and the skin deep purple, about $1^{1}/_{2}$ hours. Drain and wash well in cold water. Peel off the skin and push out the "beak" at the center where all the tentacles meet.

2. Prepare a hot charcoal fire or preheat a gas grill for 15 minutes on high.

3. Stir $1/2$ cup of the olive oil, the garlic, and parsley together. Save a couple of pinches of chopped parsley to garnish the serving platter later.

4. Place the whole precooked octopus on the grill and cook, basting with the olive oil mixture, until golden brown with crusty lavender edges, about 8 to 10 minutes. Remove and cut up the octopus into bite-size pieces.

5. Place the mussels and clams on the grill and close the cover. Grill until the shellfish open, 20 to 40 minutes. Remove from the grill and cool. Remove the shellfish from their shells and set aside.

6. Brush the squid and their tentacles with the olive oil mixture, sprinkle with salt and pepper, and place on the grill. Cook, turning and basting with the olive oil mixture, until golden, about 20 minutes. Remove, cool, and slice into rings.

7. Skewer the shrimp in their shells and brush with the olive oil mixture. Place on the grill and cook on one side for 8 minutes. Remove, lightly crush with a mallet or rolling pin, and grill until golden orange, another 8 minutes. Remove the skewers and shells. Set aside.

8. Toss all the seafood in a large bowl with the remaining $\frac{1}{2}$ cup olive oil and lemon juice to taste and add salt and pepper to taste. Arrange all the seafood attractively on a platter and sprinkle the reserved parsley over the top. Serve at room temperature.

Makes 6 servings

Grilling Seafood

If you decide to grill a lot of seafood at once and your grilling area is large enough, cooking times will increase, especially for the clams and mussels, which might take 40 minutes to open. If you like, you can steam the clams and mussels in a large pot over high heat until they open instead of grilling.

6

Vegetables and Other Foods

Grilled Red, Yellow, and Green Peppers

"Peperoni in Graticola"

Grilling bell peppers of different colors is common in Sicily and Sardinia and makes a very attractive presentation. Their flavor is a natural accompaniment to grilled meats. The charred skin of the peppers is peeled off before serving, leaving the smoky flavor. You don't have to core or halve the peppers before grilling. Photograph page 60.

2 red bell peppers

2 green bell peppers

2 yellow bell peppers

3 tablespoons olive oil

Juice of 1 lemon

2 garlic cloves, peeled and very finely chopped

2 tablespoons finely chopped fresh basil

Salt and freshly ground black pepper

1. Prepare a hot charcoal fire or preheat a gas grill for 15 minutes on high.

2. Place the peppers on the grill and cook, turning, until they are blackened on all sides, 40 to 45 minutes; remove. (Cored and halved peppers will take about the same time.) When the peppers are cool enough to handle, peel off the skin and remove the core and seeds. Cut into strips and arrange attractively on a platter.

3. Whisk together the olive oil, lemon juice, garlic, basil, and salt and pepper to taste. Pour over the peppers at the last moment and serve.

Makes 4 servings

Variation: For an even more refreshing flavor, replace the basil with an equal quantity of mint, either peppermint or spearmint.

Fired Up for Vegetables

Few people heat up a grill to cook just vegetables, so I assume that your grill will also be cooking meat or poultry. Since the heat of the grill might be low or hot, depending on the recipe you're trying, the vegetables you grill might take more or less time than suggested. This means you must pay close attention to the appearance of the food to determine doneness. A good guide is that when vegetables are golden brown, they're perfect; when you see things blackening, they're *definitely* done (except for grilled artichokes).

Grilled Stuffed Tomatoes from Sardinia

"Pomodori Arrosto sulla Griglia"

This easy recipe from Sardinia requires firm tomatoes that will not fall apart when they are grilled. The garlic flavors the bread crumbs in such a gentle way that these tomatoes make an ideal accompaniment for grilled meat. Photograph page 27.

2 garlic cloves, peeled and finely chopped

2 tablespoons finely chopped fresh parsley

3 ripe but firm tomatoes, sliced in half horizontally and seeded

Salt and freshly ground black pepper

$1/2$ cup bread crumbs

$1/2$ cup olive oil

1. Prepare a low charcoal fire or preheat a gas grill for 15 minutes on low.

2. Sprinkle the garlic and parsley on the tomatoes. Salt and pepper to taste. Sprinkle the bread crumbs on top and drizzle with olive oil. Place the tomatoes, bread crumb side up, on the grill and cook without turning until they are spotted with black on top, about 15 minutes.

Makes 3 or 4 servings

Grilled Artichokes

"Carciofi alle Brace"

As Pellegrino Artusi, the best-selling nineteenth-century Italian cookbook writer, said, "Everyone knows how to cook artichokes on a grill." If you don't, follow this recipe for a fun eating experience. My favorite Sicilian chef, Carlo Middione of Vivande Ristorante in San Francisco, roasts these whole artichokes directly in the embers of a wood fire with a sprinkle of red pepper flakes. Photograph page 57.

10 medium-size artichokes (about 4 ounces each)

¹/₂ cup olive oil

4 garlic cloves, peeled and finely chopped

3 tablespoons finely chopped fresh parsley

Salt and freshly ground black pepper

Juice of 1 lemon

1 teaspoon dried oregano (optional)

1. Prepare a medium-hot charcoal fire or preheat a gas grill for 15 minutes on medium-low.

2. Trim off the top inch and stem of each artichoke. If using baby artichokes, you can grill them with leaves and stem attached. Whisk together the olive oil, garlic, parsley, and salt and pepper to taste. Spread the leaves of the artichoke apart with your fingers or by banging the bottom on a hard surface and pour the sauce over the top, making sure it drips into all the spaces between the leaves. Alternatively, you can vertically split the artichokes in half and coat the cut sides with the dressing.

3. Place the artichokes on the grill or in the embers of the coals and cook, turning, until the outside leaves are black, if cooked on a grill, or when the bottoms of the artichokes are easily pierced with a long wooden skewer, about 45 minutes for medium-size artichokes, 25 minutes for halved or baby artichokes. Remove, drizzle with the lemon juice mixed with oregano, if using, and serve. Eat the artichokes with your hands.

Makes 8 to 10 servings

Grilled Eggplant

"Melanzane alla Griglia"

Eggplants, sometimes whole, along with scallions, artichokes, peppers, and tomatoes are a mixed vegetable grill in southern Italy. Take a look at the book cover photo and start grilling!

Three 2 1/2- to 3-pound
   eggplants, sliced lengthwise
   3/8 inch thick

Salt

1/4 cup olive oil

1 garlic clove, peeled and finely
   chopped

Freshly ground black pepper

Very good quality red wine
   vinegar

1. Lay the eggplant slices on some paper towels and sprinkle with salt. Leave them to release their bitter juices for 1 hour or longer, then pat dry with paper towels. Mix the olive oil, garlic, and salt and pepper to taste.

2. Prepare a medium-hot charcoal fire or preheat a gas grill for 15 minutes on medium-high.

3. Brush the eggplant slices with the olive oil mixture and grill until both sides are golden brown with grid marks, about 10 minutes on each side. Remove the eggplant to a platter, arrange attractively, and sprinkle with vinegar while still hot. Serve at room temperature.

Makes 6 servings

Variation 1: You can cook radicchio with the same basting sauce. Quarter the radicchio lengthwise, brush with the oil, and grill 8 minutes on each side.

Variation 2: Sprinkle the eggplant with cayenne pepper before grilling and throw some scallions on the grill too.

Variation 3: Sprinkle 1 slice of eggplant with cayenne and pecorino cheese and cover with another slice of eggplant. Secure the two with toothpicks if necessary. Baste with olive oil as they grill.

Grilled Eggplant Roll-Ups

"Braciolette di Melanzane Ripiene"

Slices of eggplant stuffed with moistened fresh bread crumbs, basil, garlic, and parsley are rolled up carefully and wrapped in thin slices of pancetta before grilling. These braciolette are the perfect accompaniment to grilled lamb or chicken.

Make sure that you do not boil the eggplants too long, or they will disintegrate when you try to roll them. When skewering, make sure that the pancetta is skewered too, so that it doesn't droop down into the fire.

1 large eggplant (about 2 pounds), cut lengthwise into 9 slices from the center, ¹/₄ inch thick

Salt and freshly ground black pepper

2 cups small bread cubes, white part only

¹/₂ cup milk

1 garlic clove, peeled and finely chopped

2 tablespoons finely chopped fresh basil

2 tablespoons finely chopped fresh parsley

1 tablespoon olive oil

9 thin slices pancetta (about ¹/₃ pound)

Eight 8- to 10-inch wooden skewers

1. Prepare a medium-hot charcoal fire or preheat a gas grill for 15 minutes on medium.

2. Drop the eggplant slices into a large saucepan of rapidly boiling water. Remove and drain as soon as the slices are soft, about 2 minutes. Dry well on paper towels. Salt and pepper to taste. Set aside.

3. Moisten the bread in the milk and then squeeze dry. Put the bread in a mixing bowl and stir in the garlic, basil, and parsley. Salt to taste and add the olive oil. Knead well.

4. Lay a slice of eggplant on a work surface. Put a heaping tablespoon of stuffing in the center and roll the eggplant up. You must roll the slices slowly and carefully, pressing any escaping stuffing back in. Wrap each eggplant roll-up in a slice of pancetta. Secure with a toothpick if necessary.

Grilled Eggplant Roll-Ups; sliced tomatoes

5. Double skewer all the ingredients: hold 2 skewers parallel to each other about ¹/₂ inch apart between your thumb and forefinger. Slide the wrapped eggplant roll-up onto the skewer, making sure you skewer the overlapping end of the eggplant and the pancetta. Put only 2 eggplant roll-ups on each set of double skewers (and 3 on the last set).

6. Place the roll-ups on the grill and cook, watching for flare-ups from the pancetta fat, for 15 minutes. Turn carefully and continue grilling until the pancetta has crispy edges and the eggplant is golden, about another 15 minutes.

Makes 4 to 6 servings

Common (Grilling) Sense

Because of the variety of grills and types of fires, I suggest that the look and feel of the food, along with the cook's common sense, be given preference over cooking times.

Grilled Portobello Mushrooms

"Funghi alla Griglia"

I find two things amazing about grilled portobello mushrooms: how much their taste and texture resemble that of meat and how perfectly they complement lamb. Try this recipe with Grilled Lamb Rib Chops (page 64), and you will see what I mean.

Any leftover grilled mushrooms can be chopped and added to a plate of spaghetti with a drizzle of extra-virgin olive oil. Photograph page 31.

6 portobello mushrooms (about 2 pounds total)

³/₄ cup finely chopped mixed fresh herbs, such as parsley, oregano, thyme, mint, basil

3 garlic cloves, peeled and finely chopped

Salt and freshly ground black pepper

1 cup olive oil

1. Prepare a hot charcoal fire or preheat a gas grill for 15 minutes on high.

2. Remove the stems of the mushrooms carefully and save for another use or grill separately. Brush, do not wash, the mushrooms. Mix the herbs, garlic, salt and pepper to taste, and olive oil and drizzle over both sides of the mushroom caps.

3. Place the mushrooms on the grill and cook, turning once or twice, until dark brown and slightly soft to the touch, about 8 minutes on each side.

Makes 4 servings

Grilled Vegetable Platter

"Grigliata di Verdure"

This platter of mixed vegetables, all grilled, is a favorite served with Mixed Grill meats (page 74). The eggplant slices in particular should have seared black grill streaks. Use them to surround the remaining grilled vegetables decoratively on the serving platter.

2 medium-size eggplants, sliced lengthwise $1/_2$ inch thick

Salt

2 fennel bulbs (about 1 $1/_2$ pounds total, trimmed of half of leafy stalks

$1/_2$ cup olive oil

3 tablespoons freshly squeezed lemon juice

1 teaspoon dried oregano

2 garlic cloves, peeled and finely chopped

3 green bell peppers

3 red bell peppers

3 yellow bell peppers

8 large basil leaves, finely chopped

Freshly ground black pepper

1. Lay the eggplant slices on some paper towels and sprinkle with salt. Leave them to release their bitter juices for 1 hour or longer, then pat dry with paper towels.

2. Meanwhile, gently boil the fennel whole in a large saucepan of lightly salted water until it can be easily punctured with a skewer, about 15 minutes. Drain and cut lengthwise into $1/_2$-inch-thick slices. If the fennel bulbs are very large, cut the slices lengthwise in half. Set aside.

3. Prepare a hot charcoal fire or preheat a gas grill for 15 minutes on medium-high. While the grill is heating, whisk together a dressing with the olive oil, lemon juice, oregano, and garlic.

4. Grill the bell peppers whole, turning occasionally, until they are blackened all over, about 40 minutes; remove. While the peppers are cooling, grill the eggplants until golden with black grid marks, about 8 minutes on each side. Grill the fennel until blackened with grid marks, about 6 minutes on each side.

5. When the peppers are cool enough to handle, peel off the skin and remove the core and seeds. Cut into strips or quarters and arrange attractively on a large platter. Arrange the eggplants and fennel on the serving platter.

6. Pour the dressing over the vegetables, sprinkle with basil and salt and pepper to taste, and serve at room temperature.

Makes 8 servings

Variation: Enlarge the platter by also grilling red onions, zucchini, radicchio, and artichokes.

Vegetable Grilling 101

Vegetables should be brushed with olive oil and cooked slowly over low to medium coals/heat. After grilling, drizzle with extra-virgin olive oil if desired.

Grilled Onions

"Cipolle sulla Gratella"

A grilled onion is surprisingly sweet; the hint of caramelization goes well with grilled meats.

For variation, use other herbs, such as thyme, sage, or oregano, or sprinkle with red pepper. Photograph page 43.

3 medium-size to large yellow onions (about 2 pounds), peeled

¼ cup olive oil

3 tablespoons finely chopped fresh parsley

Salt and freshly ground black pepper

1. Prepare a hot charcoal fire or preheat a gas grill for 15 minutes on high.

2. Meanwhile, gently boil the onions whole in a large saucepan of lightly salted water for 10 minutes. Drain and cut into halves or quarters. Dip the onions in a bath made of olive oil, parsley, and salt and pepper to taste.

3. Grill the onions, turning, until they are browned and easily pierced with a fork, about 30 minutes.

Makes 6 servings

Variation: Use 2 pounds of peeled red onions.

Grilled Polenta

"Polenta alla Griglia"

Polenta is traditionally made in an all-copper concave cauldron called a paioli. *The corn-meal is always stirred in one direction for almost an hour. The method of cooking polenta that I use, just as good and much easier than the traditional method, was developed by my friend Carlo Middione, the chef/owner of Vivande Ristorante in San Francisco and author of* The Food of Southern Italy. *Photograph page 106.*

2 quarts water

1 tablespoon salt

2 cups cornmeal

1. In the bottom half of a double boiler, pour enough water to reach and cover the bottom of the top part. Bring this water to a boil over high heat and then reduce the heat to medium-low, so that the water is just under a bubble.

2. Bring 2 quarts of water to a boil in the top part of the double boiler. Add the salt.

3. Using a wooden spoon, stir the water in the top part of the double boiler until you've created a whirlpool. Now pour the cornmeal into the center of the whirlpool in a continuous steady stream, not too fast, not too slow. Do not stop stirring. Continue to stir at a slower pace once the cornmeal is in the pot. Reduce the heat to low and stir while the polenta bubbles slightly until it thickens, 3 to 5 minutes.

4. Place the lid on the top part and fit the top part over the bottom of the double boiler. Cook, stirring every 30 minutes, for 1¹/₂ hours. Taste. If the polenta is bitter, cook longer.

5. Pour the polenta out onto an oiled butcher block or baking tray, spread until 1 inch thick, and let cool at room temperature. When completely cool cut into 4 × 3-inch rectangles or, if you prefer, cut into triangles.

6. While the polenta is cooling, prepare a hot charcoal fire or preheat a gas grill for 15 minutes on high.

7. Brush the polenta on both sides with olive oil and grill until golden with black grid marks, about 8 minutes on each side.

Makes 8 servings

Grilled Stale Bread

"Bruschetta"

Bruschetta *(pronounced broos-KET-ta) is a grilled bread now popular throughout this country. Originally, grilling was a way to use up old bread. So this recipe might sound ridiculous, but you will be amazed at how a slice of stale Italian bread, when dipped in warm water and placed on the grill, is not only edible but extraordinary. The principle is the same for Red Slice (page 173), which is an even better but slightly more involved recipe.*

4 large slices 2-day-old round Italian or French country bread

Tepid water as needed

Extra-virgin olive oil for drizzling

1. Prepare a hot charcoal fire or preheat a gas grill for 15 minutes on high.

2. Very quickly dip both sides of the stale bread in a pan filled with tepid water. Place on the grill, and when one side has even grid marks, turn to other side and grill until no longer soggy, 5 to 10 minutes. Transfer to a serving platter and drizzle with olive oil.

Makes 4 servings

Variation: You can use fresh bread too, in which case do not dip in water before grilling.

Italian Vegetable Grilling, or *Abbrustolire*!

The Italians use a special word for grilling vegetables or bread: *abbrustolire,* which means grilling over fire. The most popular vegetables grilled by Italians are bell peppers, eggplants, and mushrooms. Tomatoes, leeks, scallions, onions, artichokes, cardoons, fennel, and radicchio are also grilled, and in some parts of the country even more unusual vegetables. For instance, in some areas of Apulia, chickpeas are dusted with cayenne pepper and roasted in a fire pit built in the sand, called *la muertaciadda*. In other parts of Italy, *muscari,* a dialect word for grape hyacinth bulbs, are boiled with vinegar and then grilled.

Grilled bread, *bruschetta,* is a popular preparation when doused with extra-virgin olive oil and seared lightly.

Red Slice

"Fédda Rossa"

In Apulia they grill stale bread, then dunk it in water and grill it a second time. The bread is covered with tomatoes and salt—hence the name fédda rossa, *dialect for "red slice."*

I always have fédda rossa *ready for a summertime grill. It's terrific for staving off hungry hordes. As simple as this is, the memory of the flavors will stay with you long after you taste them.*

1 large loaf 2-day-old round Italian or French country bread, sliced

Extra-virgin olive oil

Salt and freshly ground black pepper

1 1/2 pounds very ripe tomatoes, chopped and drained

1. Prepare a hot charcoal fire or preheat a gas grill for 15 minutes on high.

2. Put the bread slices on the grill and cook until they brown, then turn and brown the other sides, 5 to 10 minutes total.

3. Dip the whole slices of grilled bread into a shallow baking pan filled with water for 2 seconds on each side, then return to the grill until the bread dries out, 5 to 10 minutes.

4. Sprinkle the bread with olive oil, salt, lots of freshly ground black pepper, and the tomatoes.

Makes 8 servings

7

Pasta and Salad
Accompaniments

Spaghetti with Red Chili Pepper

Absolutely perfect with grilled fish! In the summertime this simple preparation should be allowed to rest until it no longer steams. Photograph page 128.

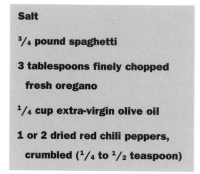

Salt

³/₄ pound spaghetti

3 tablespoons finely chopped
    fresh oregano

¹/₄ cup extra-virgin olive oil

1 or 2 dried red chili peppers,
    crumbled (¹/₄ to ¹/₂ teaspoon)

1. Bring a large pot of water to a rolling boil, salt abundantly, and add the pasta. Drain when al dente.

2. Toss the spaghetti with the oregano, olive oil, and red chili pepper. Transfer to a serving platter. Let sit 10 minutes before serving.

Makes 4 servings

An Americanization

Traditionally, Italians eat pasta as a first course to be followed by a grilled dish. Although all the grill recipes are authentic and traditional, this chapter offers pasta and salad accompaniments to those dishes rather than *primi piatti,* first courses. So my apologies to the purists for this Americanization.

Spaghetti with Parsley and Anchovy

This preparation—the height of simplicity—is typically served before or with grilled fish. Photograph page 132.

Salt

1 pound spaghetti

¹/₄ to ¹/₂ teaspoon red chili pepper flakes

3 tablespoons finely chopped fresh parsley

¹/₄ cup olive oil

3 garlic cloves, peeled and very finely chopped

8 salted anchovy fillets, rinsed and finely chopped

1. Bring a large pot of water to a rolling boil, salt abundantly, and add the pasta. Drain when al dente.

2. Meanwhile, combine the red chili flakes, parsley, olive oil, garlic, and anchovies in a small frying pan. Cook over low heat, stirring frequently to keep the garlic from burning, until the anchovies are completely melted, about 6 minutes.

3. Toss the sauce with the spaghetti and serve.

Makes 4 servings

Cool Accompaniments

I assume that most people grill more in the summer than in the winter. For this reason the pasta and salad chapter consists of food served lukewarm or at room temperature. In the winter, serve it hot if desired.

Fettuccelle with Tomato Sauce, Olives, and Capers

"Fettuccelle alla Pugliese"

This aromatic sauce is typical of calzone stuffings in Apulia. Here it is tossed with fettuccelle, a pasta wider than fettuccine. The dish complements grilled tuna or swordfish.

Salt

1 pound fettuccelle or fettuccine

$^1/_4$ cup olive oil

1 pound white onions, peeled and sliced

2 cups chopped ripe tomatoes (about 1 pound)

$^2/_3$ cup chopped imported black olives

1 tablespoon capers

6 salted anchovy fillets, rinsed and chopped

2 tablespoons finely chopped fresh parsley

$^1/_4$ pound pecorino cheese, cut into tiny cubes (about 1 cup)

1. Bring a large pot of water to a rolling boil, salt abundantly, and add the pasta. Drain when al dente.

2. Meanwhile, heat the olive oil in a large frying pan over medium heat. Add the onions and cook, stirring, until they are soft and turning color, 12 to 15 minutes. Add the tomatoes, olives, capers, anchovies, and parsley. Mix well and salt to taste. Cook until the tomatoes are blended and the anchovies melted, about 10 minutes.

3. Raise the heat to high, add the pecorino, and cook, stirring and mixing, until the pecorino begins to get stringy, 2 to 3 minutes. Remove the pan from the heat and transfer the sauce to a large bowl. Toss with the pasta. Leave for 10 minutes and serve.

Makes 4 to 6 servings

Tagliatelle with Garlic, Olive Oil, and Raw Tomatoes

"Tagliatelle Aglio e Olio con Pomodoro Crudo"

*T*his is a quick preparation for a summer accompaniment to grilled tuna. The "sauce" is crudo, *that is, raw, and will be all the better with fresh tagliatelle if you can find it or make it yourself. Photograph page 144.*

1 pound ripe tomatoes, seeded and sliced into small slivers

$^1/_2$ cup extra-virgin olive oil

3 to 4 large garlic cloves, peeled and finely chopped

2 tablespoons finely chopped fresh parsley

Salt

1 pound tagliatelle

Freshly ground black pepper

1. Put the tomato slivers in a strainer and drain for 2 hours.

2. Combine the olive oil in a small saucepan with the garlic and parsley. Gently warm the oil over very low heat, never letting it cook or sizzle.

3. Bring a large pot of water to a rolling boil, salt abundantly, and add the pasta. Drain when al dente and toss with the olive oil mixture and drained tomatoes. Sprinkle with some black pepper and serve.

Makes 4 servings

Variation: Use fresh basil instead of parsley and/or use thin slices of roasted yellow bell pepper with or instead of the tomatoes. Add red chili pepper flakes for some bite.

Warm Spaghetti with Sun-Dried Tomatoes and Fresh Goat Cheese

After the spaghetti is drained, toss it with the other ingredients and let their flavors meld slowly as the pasta cools from hot to warm. You will need only a small portion if you serve it with Grilled Lamb Rib Chops (page 64) and Grilled Portobello Mushrooms (page 163).

Salt

1/2 pound spaghetti

4 slices sun-dried tomatoes, soaked in water for 30 minutes (soaking is not necessary if they are oil-packed)

1/4 cup olive oil

1 tablespoon finely chopped mixed fresh herbs, such as parsley, oregano, thyme, mint, basil

2 garlic cloves, peeled and finely chopped

3 ounces soft goat cheese

Freshly ground black pepper

1. Bring a large pot of water to a rolling boil, salt abundantly, and add the pasta. Drain when al dente.

2. Meanwhile, drain the tomatoes and chop. (You should have about 3 tablespoons.) Toss with the olive oil, mixed herbs, garlic, goat cheese, and black pepper to taste.

3. Toss the spaghetti with the other ingredients until they are well mixed and transfer to a serving platter. Leave for 15 minutes before serving.

Makes 4 servings

Grilled Shark and Anaheim Peppers with Penne, Tomatoes, and Basil

This preparation is a piatto unico, *a one-pot meal that should be served in an attractive large serving bowl.*

6 tablespoons olive oil, plus additional for dipping

1 garlic clove, peeled and finely chopped

2 tablespoons finely chopped fresh basil

2 ripe plum tomatoes, coarsely chopped

Salt

³/₄ pound penne

Four 10-inch wooden skewers

1 pound shark steaks, ¹/₂ inch thick, cut into 1-inch squares

6 Anaheim (long green) chili peppers, seeded and cut into 1-inch pieces

Freshly ground black pepper

1. Prepare a hot charcoal fire or preheat a gas grill for 15 minutes on high. Mix 6 tablespoons olive oil, the garlic, basil, and tomatoes together.

2. Bring a large pot of water to a rolling boil, salt abundantly, and add the pasta. Drain when al dente.

3. Meanwhile, skewer the fish and Anaheim peppers, dip the skewers in olive oil, and salt and pepper to taste. Place on the grill and cook, turning once, until the fish has black grid marks, about 8 minutes on each side.

4. Toss the penne with the tomato mixture. Pull the fish and peppers off the skewers and toss with the penne. Or leave on the skewers and serve on top of the pasta.

Makes 4 servings

Grilled Shark and Anaheim Peppers with Penne, Tomatoes, and Basil; tossed salad

Pappardelle with Rabbit Sauce

"Pappardelle con Sugo di Coniglio"

This preparation utilizes all the rabbit bones you've saved from making Grilled Rabbit and Sausage Skewers, Molise Style (page 78). This is a very nice sauce best tossed with fresh pappardelle, a pasta about ½ inch in width. In its place use tagliatelle or fettuccine.

1 pound rabbit bones

6 cups cold water

1 small onion, peeled, quartered, and separated

1 small carrot, sliced

¹/₂ rib celery, sliced

5 black peppercorns

Bouquet garni: 6 sprigs fresh parsley and 3 sprigs fresh oregano tied in cheesecloth

3 tablespoons olive oil

¹/₄ cup very finely chopped onion

3 tablespoons white wine

1 garlic clove, peeled and crushed

Salt

³/₄ pound fresh pappardelle, tagliatelle, or fettuccine

¹/₄ cup freshly grated parmesan cheese

1. Put the rabbit bones, cold water, onion, carrot, celery, peppercorns, and bouquet garni in a 4-quart pot and bring to a boil over high heat. Skim the surface of foam. Reduce the heat to very low and simmer for 6 hours. Strain, discarding all the bones and vegetables. There is no need to defat the stock because rabbit is so lean there is no significant fat. Set aside until needed.

2. Heat the olive oil in a large saucepan over medium-high heat. Add the chopped onion and cook, stirring frequently, until golden, about 4 minutes. Pour in the wine and let it almost evaporate, about 1 minute. Pour in the reserved rabbit stock and the garlic and cook until the liquid reduces to about ³/₄ cup, 30 to 35 minutes.

3. Meanwhile, bring a large pot of water to a rolling boil, salt abundantly, and add the pasta. Drain when al dente and transfer to the saucepan. Toss well with the rabbit sauce and sprinkle with the parmesan cheese, tossing well.

Makes 4 servings

Russian Salad

"Insalata Russa"

*T*his popular salad is often served as an appetizer on outdoor banquet tables, fuori tavola, in trattorias, where one finds innumerable delicious tidbits. This is a simple recipe that goes well with grilled beef. A more involved preparation is given in the variation below.

Salt

1 cup diced carrots (about 6 ounces)

2 cups fresh or frozen shelled peas (about 10 ounces)

$^1/_2$ cup mayonnaise, commercial or homemade (page 198)

1. Bring a pot of lightly salted water to a boil, add the carrots, and cook until tender, about 5 minutes. Add the peas and cook until tender, about another 5 minutes. Drain well.

2. When the peas and carrots are completely cool and well drained, stir in the mayonnaise with a spoon. Mound attractively on a serving platter. The vegetables should hold together with the mayonnaise.

Makes 4 servings (Variation makes 8 servings)

Variation: Add some or all of the following: 1 cup diced cooked turnips, 1 cup diced cooked potatoes, 1 cup chopped cooked lobster meat. Decorate with $^1/_2$ cup diced baked small young beets (baked whole for 40 minutes in a 350°F oven, then peeled). Stir 1 finely chopped gherkin, 1 tablespoon finely chopped capers, and 2 salted anchovy fillets, rinsed and finely chopped, into 1 cup mayonnaise.

Perfect Partners

Throughout the book, the general recommendation for accompaniments, whether indicated in the recipe or not, is pasta or rice before or with fish and shellfish, grilled vegetables and salads before or with meat, and either or both with poultry.

Seafood Rice Salad

"Riso di Mare"

I first had this wonderful rice salad al fresco in the tiny Sicilian port of San Gregorio, after a day of strenuous skin diving. It was heaven enough, and then came the grilled fish (pages 110 to 142).

For a less traditional but more dramatic presentation, decorate the salad with a few of the cooked mussels and clams in their shells.

6 mussels, scrubbed and
   debearded just before cooking

6 littleneck clams, scrubbed

1/2 carrot, peeled

1 squid, cleaned

3 tablespoons butter

2 1/2 cups medium-grain
   (Spanish) white rice

2 1/2 cups water

Salt

6 cooked medium-size shrimp,
   shelled and very finely
   chopped

One 3-ounce can Italian tuna
   packed in oil, very finely
   chopped with oil

3 ounces Norwegian or Scottish
   smoked salmon, very finely
   chopped

1. Place the mussels and clams in a pot with a few table-spoons of water and turn the heat to high. Cover and cook until they open, about 4 to 6 minutes. Discard any that do not open. Let the mussels and clams cool, remove from their shells, and chop very finely. Set aside in a medium-size mixing bowl.

2. Place the carrot in a small saucepan, cover with water, and turn the heat to high. Bring to a boil and cook until crisp-tender (or whatever you prefer), about 10 minutes. Drain and chop very finely.

3. Put the squid in the pot in which you cooked the mollusks. Add 3 tablespoons water and cook on high heat until firm, about 4 minutes. Let cool and chop very finely. Cut the tentacles in half and set aside. Add the rest of the chopped squid to the mixing bowl with the clams and mussels.

4. Melt the butter in a heavy 4-quart enameled cast-iron pot or casserole with a heavy lid over medium-high heat. Add the rice and cook, stirring frequently, for

2 canned hearts of palm,
   drained and very finely
   chopped

2 teaspoons beluga or salmon
   caviar (or ¹/₂ teaspoon black
   or red lumpfish caviar)

1 tablespoon very finely
   chopped fresh parsley

3 tablespoons olive oil

Freshly ground black pepper

Parsley sprigs for garnish

3 minutes. Add the water and 2 teaspoons of salt, reduce the heat to very low, cover, and cook undisturbed for 12 minutes. Do not lift the lid until then. Check to see if the rice is cooked and all the water has been absorbed. If it isn't, add a little boiling water and cook until tender. Transfer the cooked rice to a large mixing bowl, spreading it out so it will cool faster.

5. Once the rice has completely cooled, use a fork to toss it very well with the mussels, clams, squid, shrimp, tuna, smoked salmon, carrot, hearts of palm, caviar, parsley, and olive oil. Check for seasoning and add salt and pepper if needed.

6. Arrange attractively on an oval platter and garnish each end with the squid tentacles and parsley sprigs.

Makes 6 servings

Neapolitan-Style Tomato Salad

"Insalata di Pomodori alla Napoletana"

Neapolitans make this tomato salad with large tomatoes that still have a little green on them. This recipe uses ripe ones and makes a great salad for a large grill party. At no time should tomatoes be refrigerated. Photograph page 81.

14 large ripe tomatoes (7 to 8 pounds total), cut in half

Dressing:

³/₄ cup olive oil

¹/₄ cup red wine vinegar, or to taste

4 garlic cloves, peeled and finely chopped

3 tablespoons finely chopped fresh basil

1 teaspoon dried oregano

Salt and freshly ground black pepper

1. Seed the tomatoes and cut into thin wedges. Place in a colander and leave to drain for 2 hours.

2. For the dressing, whisk together the olive oil, vinegar, garlic, basil, and oregano.

3. Transfer the drained tomatoes to a large mixing bowl and toss with the vinaigrette. Salt and pepper to taste. Serve at room temperature.

Makes 10 to 12 servings

A Whimsical Salad of Artichoke, Celery, and Peas

"Insalata di Carciofi, Sedano, e Piselli Capricciosa in Bianco Speciale"

This is a special preparation, traditionally served as an antipasto but perfect, too, for a spring dinner with Grilled Lamb Rib Chops (page 64). I also like to serve this salad with any of the grilled involtini.

1/4 cup all-purpose flour

2 quarts cold water

2 teaspoons salt

Juice of 1 lemon

1/4 cup unsalted butter

8 fresh artichoke hearts

4 cups sliced celery hearts

2 cups fresh or frozen shelled peas

1/2 cup mayonnaise, commercial or homemade (page 198)

2 sprigs fresh curly parsley

2 hard-boiled large eggs, quartered

1. Put the flour, water, salt, lemon juice, and butter in a large enameled pot and bring to a boil. Add the artichoke hearts and cook over medium-high heat until al dente, about 5 minutes. Remove the artichoke hearts and slice thinly. Add the sliced celery hearts and peas to the boiling broth. Return the sliced artichoke hearts and boil until tender, about 8 minutes. Drain all the vegetables well, discarding the broth, and set aside until completely cooled.

2. Toss the vegetables with the mayonnaise and check the seasoning. Arrange on a serving platter and decorate with parsley sprigs. Arrange the eggs around the platter and serve.

Makes 4 to 6 servings

8

Sauces and Marinades

Warm Olive Oil and Oregano Sauce

"Sammurigghiu"

Many people who love Italian food know this Sicilian sauce for fish by its Italian name, salmoriglio. It comes from the Sicilian word sammurigghiu, *literally meaning "brine." In fact this is no brine, but rather a delicious bath for fresh grilled fish or even steak. With the addition of some tomato, it becomes* rosso, red. *The recipe is very simple, just a whisking together of olive oil, lemon juice, garlic, and herbs in a double boiler. Photograph page 200.*

¹/₂ cup olive oil

Juice of 1 lemon

2 tablespoons hot water

Salt and freshly ground black pepper

2 tablespoons very finely chopped fresh oregano or 1 teaspoon dried

6 tablespoons very finely chopped fresh parsley

2 garlic cloves, peeled and very finely chopped

Pour an inch or so of water into the bottom of a double boiler and bring to a boil. Set the top part in place. Pour the olive oil into the top of the double boiler and slowly whisk in the lemon juice and hot water. Season with salt and pepper to taste and then whisk in the oregano, parsley, and garlic. Cook, whisking constantly, until the flavors are blended, about 5 minutes. Remove from the heat and keep warm. Use the sauce to baste or pour over fish or meat after grilling.

Makes about ¾ cup

Orange and Oregano Marinade

"Marinato d'Arancio e Origano"

This marinade is perfect for swordfish and very nice with cuts of beef such as skirt steak or sirloin tip or with pork tenderloin.

¹/₄ cup olive oil

Juice of 1 large orange

1 tablespoon dried oregano

1 to 2 garlic cloves, peeled and finely chopped

Mix all the ingredients together and use to marinate the fish or beef in the refrigerator, covered, for 2 hours. Remove the food from the refrigerator 15 minutes before grilling.

Makes ½ to ¾ cup marinade (enough for 1 to 1½ pounds fish, beef, or pork)

Pesto

"Pesto alla Genovese"

*P*esto is made by pounding fresh basil, pine nuts, garlic, and parmesan cheese in a mortar. It is so popular and well-known it is sold in most supermarkets in jars. But it is not time-consuming to make from scratch, so I recommend you try the extraordinary taste of freshly made pesto. I continue to make pesto by hand rather than with a food processor.

Fresh basil leaves should be pounded gently rather than processed. The pesto should be a heavy, thick puree after you add the olive oil. The highest-quality extra-virgin olive oil is essential. This recipe will give you a fairly liquid pesto with a mild garlic flavor. To make it stronger and thicker, use ¾ cup olive oil and 4 garlic cloves. Store in a jar in the refrigerator and let it come to room temperature when using.

1 bunch fresh basil (50 to 60 medium to large leaves), washed and thoroughly dried

2 large garlic cloves, peeled

Pinch of salt

2 tablespoons pine nuts, toasted (see Note)

3 tablespoons freshly grated parmesan cheese

3 tablespoons freshly grated pecorino cheese

1 cup extra-virgin olive oil

1. There should be no water on the basil leaves. Use a salad spinner to remove the water from the washed basil, then damp dry with paper towels. Place the basil, garlic cloves, salt, and pine nuts in a marble mortar and begin gently crushing with the pestle. Once the basil begins to become mushy, pound more, pressing the leaves clinging to the sides down into the center of the mortar. Pound gently so that you make the pesto into a paste, not a liquid. Slowly add the cheeses about a tablespoon every minute and continue pounding. You should be pounding about 9 to 12 minutes.

2. Once the pesto is a thick paste, scrape it into a large, deep, heavy ceramic bowl and slowly begin to pour in the olive oil, stirring constantly with the back of a wooden spoon or continuing to use the pestle.

Makes 1½ cups

Note: To toast pine nuts, spread them on a baking sheet and bake in a 350°F oven, stirring once, until golden, 5 to 7 minutes.

Devil's Hot Sauce

"Salsa alla Diavola"

I adapted this famous old sauce from Ada Boni, the noted Italian cookbook writer of the mid-twentieth century. It's used with lobster, shrimp, or firm-fleshed fish. Photograph page 200.

$^1/_2$ **cup white wine vinegar**

Pinch of freshly ground black pepper

2 dried red chili peppers

1 tablespoon tomato paste

1 cup beef bouillon

1 tablespoon all-purpose flour

1 tablespoon butter

1 teaspoon Dijon mustard

1. Pour the vinegar into a small saucepan and add the black pepper and red chili pepper. Bring to a boil over high heat and cook until the vinegar reduces by half, about 3 minutes.

2. Dissolve the tomato paste in the beef bouillon and add to the vinegar. Reduce the heat to low and cook at a gentle boil for 10 minutes.

3. Form a *burro maneggiato* by blending the flour and butter with a fork, then beat into the sauce. Remove from the heat and stir in the mustard. Remove and discard the red chili peppers before using.

Makes about 1 cup

Mayonnaise

"Maionese"

I include this recipe for mayonnaise because homemade is so much better than store-bought. Mayonnaise is a great accompaniment to many foods but has a sullied reputation because of misuse.

³/₄ cup light olive oil

³/₄ cup vegetable oil

1 large egg (see Note)

1 tablespoon freshly squeezed lemon juice or good-quality white wine vinegar

¹/₂ teaspoon very fine salt

¹/₂ teaspoon very finely ground white pepper

Mix the oils together. Put the egg in a food processor and run for 30 seconds. Slowly pour in the oil in a very thin stream with the processor running, about 6 minutes of pouring. Blend in the lemon juice or vinegar for 30 seconds. Add the salt and pepper and continue blending for 30 seconds. Refrigerate for 1 hour before using.

Makes 2 cups

Note: If you are concerned about possible salmonella contamination in raw eggs, substitute a good-quality mayonnaise.

Mayonnaise Stories

Mayonnaise is said to have originated in the capital city of Mahon in the Balearic Islands. One story concerning the origins of mayonnaise holds that Marshal Richelieu, the grandnephew of the infamous cardinal, after expelling the British from Minorca in 1756, was out walking in the countryside and grew hungry. He asked a local peasant woman to make something for him, and realizing that he was important, she improvised a sauce from the few precious eggs she had been hoarding.

Another story says that King Carlos III of Spain stopped in Mao on his way from Barcelona to Naples in 1760 and was feted by the local governor. The banquet featured lobster, for which Minorca is famous, simply grilled. It didn't look appetizing to the king, so the governor ordered the kitchen to make a sauce instantly.

Mixed Mayonnaise for Grilled Fish or Chicken

"Salsa Gremolada"

Mayonnaise has declined in popularity over the years and is rarely associated with Italian cuisine. In fact, the Italians use mayonnaise a lot in everything from panini, *little sandwiches, to this* salsa gremolada, *which is a perfectly fine accompaniment to grilled fish, as long as you use it in moderation. Make sure the parsley is completely dry before you chop it. Photograph page 200.*

1 ¹/₂ cups mayonnaise, commercial or homemade (page 198)

2 tablespoons very finely chopped fresh parsley

3 sweet gherkins, dried and finely chopped

1 tablespoon finely chopped capers, rinsed and dried well

1 scallion (green onion), white part only, very finely chopped

1 teaspoon mustard

1 teaspoon anchovy paste

1. Prepare the fresh mayonnaise, if using.

2. Whisk in the parsley, gherkins, capers, scallion, mustard, and anchovy paste. Taste and correct for salt and pepper.

Makes 1½ cups

(clockwise from top spoon) Warm Olive Oil and Oregano Sauce (page 194); Sauce for Grilled Fish (page 202); Devil's Hot Sauce (page 197); Mixed Mayonnaise for Grilled Fish or Chicken

Sauce for Grilled Fish

"Salsa peril Pesce"

The eggs make for a rich mayonnaise, so you can use this old and traditional dressing for fish sparingly. Photograph page 200.

4 large eggs (see Note, page 198), 3 hard-boiled

6 salted anchovy fillets, rinsed

1 ½ cups olive oil

Juice of ½ lemon

Salt and freshly ground black pepper

1. Remove the yolks from the hard-boiled eggs and mash them in a mortar with the anchovy fillets until well blended. Discard the whites or save for another use.

2. Place the remaining uncooked egg in a food processor and run for 30 seconds. Add the egg yolk and anchovy mixture to the food processor and blend with a few short pulses. With the food processor running, slowly add the olive oil in a continuous thin stream, about 6 minutes of pouring. Add the lemon juice and blend for 30 seconds. Salt and pepper to taste and blend for a few seconds more.

Makes 2 cups

Index

Note: Page numbers in **boldface** refer to illustrations.